STRESS
&
Health

Behavioral Medicine and Health Psychology Series

Behavioral Medicine and Health Psychology brings the latest advances in these fields directly into undergraduate, graduate, and professional classrooms via individual texts that each present one topic in a self-contained manner. The texts also allow health professionals specializing in one field to become familiar with another by reading the appropriate volume, a task facilitated by their short length and their scholarly yet accessible format.

The development of the series is guided by its Editorial Board, which comprises experts from the disciplines of experimental and clinical psychology, medicine and preventive medicine, psychiatry and behavioral sciences, nursing, public health, biobehavioral health, behavioral health sciences, and behavioral genetics. Board members are based in North America, Europe, and Australia, thereby providing a truly international perspective on current research and clinical practice in behavioral medicine and health psychology.

EDITORIAL BOARD

Books in This Series

Stress & Health: Biological and Psychological Interactions,
    by William R. Lovallo

STRESS
&
Health

Biological and
Psychological Interactions

William R. Lovallo

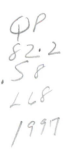

SAGE Publications
International Educational and Professional Publisher
Thousand Oaks   London   New Delhi

For information, address to:

SAGE Publications, Inc.
2455 Teller Road
Thousand Oaks, California 91320
E-mail: order@sagepub.com

SAGE Publications Ltd.
6 Bonhill Street
London EC2A 4PU
United Kingdom

SAGE Publications India Pvt. Ltd.
M-32 Market
Greater Kailash I
New Delhi 110 048 India

Printed in the United States of America

Library of Congress Cataloging-in-Publication Data

Lovallo, William R.
    Stress & health: Biological and psychological
  interactions / William R. Lovallo
      p. cm. — (Behavioral medicine and health psychology; vol. 1)
    Includes bibliographical references and index.
    ISBN 0-8039-7000-5 (cloth: alk. paper).—ISBN 0-8039-7001-3
  (pbk.: alk. paper)
    1. Stress (Physiology)   2. Stress (Psychology)   3. Clinical health psychology.
  I. Title. II. Series.

QP82.2.S8L68   1997
616.9′8—dc20   96-35626

97 98 99 00 01 02 03 10 9 8 7 6 5 4 3 2 1

Acquiring Editor:	C. Deborah Laughton
Editorial Assistant:	Eileen Carr
Production Editor:	Sanford Robinson
Production Assistant:	Denise Santoyo
Typesetter/Designer:	Marion Warren
Indexer:	Janet Perlman
Cover Designer:	Ravi Balasuriya
Print Buyer:	Anna Chin

Contents

Series Editor's Introduction

Stress & Health: Biological and Psychological Interactions discusses how interactions between mind and body may play a role in disease etiology and also, therefore, in health promotion. This topic has been of long-standing interest to philosophers, physicians, and scholars, and Professor Lovallo provides a fascinating historical perspective on the evolution of our thoughts and theories in this arena across two millennia. What makes this text unique, however, is the way in which it concurrently introduces the biological systems that facilitate mind-body interactions and shows in contemporary neurobiological terms how an idea can exert influence over our bodies.

In his classic monograph "Cardiovascular Psychophysiology: A Perspective," published by Plenum Press in 1981, the late Professor Paul Obrist challenged us to become better biologists in order to understand more completely the mechanisms through which psychological input might affect our physiology. Dr. Lovallo has risen to this challenge, providing us with a superb integration of neurobiology, psychology, immunology, and medicine.

The following chapters, then, explore how our thoughts and other psychological processes can alter our physical health in a detrimental manner. Stress is employed as the ideal vehicle for this exploration, since it "forces us to consider how our perceptions and interpretations of the world can result in negative emotions and how these can change the autonomic and endocrine influences on the rest of the body" (p. 165). As well as integrating a wide variety of factual information, this volume makes a major conceptual contribution, since it represents a reframed way of understanding "our nature as living beings whose behavior is not separate from our physical makeup and whose health is not separate from our thoughts and emotions" (p. 178).

Throughout his presentation, Dr. Lovallo has employed sound educational principles to maximize comprehension, retention, and enjoyment of the text. Its purpose and organization are made clear at the outset, and ideas and facts are developed and introduced in a logical, stepwise fashion. Individual chapters contain summaries and lists of further readings, and the volume concludes with an integrative review that also points the way for future research. Also incorporated in the text are 20 figures, including several exquisite flow diagrams that encapsulate complex processes with exceptional clarity and elegance.

Several factors fell nicely into place as this volume assumed a pivotal role in the development of the series. As well as maintaining his own distinguished research career at the University of Oklahoma, Dr. Lovallo is Associate Director of the John D. and Catherine T. MacArthur Foundation's Research Network on Mind-Body Interactions. His work in the latter capacity gives him access to the very latest research in many of the world's leading laboratories investigating these issues. When we first met in San Francisco to discuss this project, I was looking for first-rate scientists and authors to write for the series, and Dr. Lovallo was looking for a suitable publishing format for his thoughts on stress and health. This literary symbiosis led directly to the present volume.

Since this lead volume introduces the series, several acknowledgments are in order. David Ragland and Len Syme gave me the academic freedom to instigate the series during my time with them in the School of Public Health at the University of California, Berkeley. C. Deborah Laughton, my editor at Sage, is a constant source of excellent counsel, and the Editorial Board members also contribute invaluably. Thanks are extended to all of these collaborators.

Finally, I should like to express my thanks to Dr. Lovallo for the expertise, creativity, and dedication he has given to the preparation of the present text. When you have read it, I sincerely believe you will agree that it is an outstanding work.

J. Rick Turner
Chapel Hill, North Carolina

Preface

This book is an introduction to the concept of psychological stress, its physiological mechanisms, and its effects on health and disease.

When I told a former student that I was writing a book on stress, she replied, "What, *another* book on stress?" The topic of stress is widely covered in both the lay media and academia, and the reader may well ask why we need another book on the subject. There are two reasons.

First, it is widely believed that stress is a significant factor in each of our lives and that it may contribute to illness. This view has a history going back at least a century, and it is a guiding principle in the field of health psychology. For this reason, it seems timely and useful to make available a readable account of the specific linkages between emotions and physiological changes.

Second, in reviewing books and papers available to the student and the general professional audience, I noted a lack of integrated texts dealing with the question of how physiological mechanisms are affected during psychological stress. Instead, the material is often highly specialized or appears scattered in review articles and chapters. This fragmentation places an undue burden on the reader to assemble a wide range of incompatible materials written for varying purposes and often along narrowly focused lines. As a result, it becomes unnecessarily difficult for students and working professionals to develop a feel for the pathways by which thoughts and emotions affect the body.

This book evolved from a course I taught at the University of Oklahoma Health Sciences Center on Stress and Disease. That course stemmed from my interest in helping graduate students in biological psychology understand how stress affects the body and may alter long-term health. Most important, I sensed the need to attend carefully to the biological links between how we think and feel and potential alterations in health. As a result, this book concentrates on the psychophysiological linkages among cognition, emotion, and the brain and peripheral mechanisms by which the body is regulated.

A second interest I had in my course was to enhance the integration of the concept of stress by presenting the idea in its historical context and in relation to the development of medicine. Although we have an increasingly clear understanding of the machinery of the body and its systemic dysregulation in disease, medicine is lacking in a conceptual approach to understanding how social processes and emotions can improve or worsen health. I therefore start and finish here with a brief historical discussion of the mind-body relationship in terms of the development of the current system of medicine. Exposure to these broader questions will provide students with a more complete feel for the potential contributions that behavioral medicine can make to the study of health and disease.

This presentation is intended for undergraduate and graduate students of psychology, physiology, psychophysiology, behavioral medicine, and neuro-immunology who are interested in a broad introduction to these topics. There will also be selected areas in which more advanced students may find new information or a useful review. I assume that most readers will have a background in psychology and at least one course in physiological psychology and related aspects of biology. Chapters 4 through 9 presume an exposure to human neuroanatomy, neurophysiology, and some autonomic and endocrine physiology. For readers lacking such background preparation, I have avoided the use of specialized terms without explanation and I have referred to background sources where it seemed appropriate.

This book should be useful in basic courses in health psychology for undergraduates and graduates alike. It may serve as a stand-alone text or as a basis for more extensive coverage of each topic, supplemented by appropriate readings. Finally, this book should also serve the professional wishing to review the topic of psychological stress and health.

The material here is intended to help the reader understand the central nervous system mechanisms connecting our thoughts and emotions to our autonomic and endocrine processes. This book therefore is intended as a short review of how our behaviors, especially ideas and associated emotions, come to have power over our bodies. In the process, it is my hope that the reader will gain some useful insights into how an understanding of psychological processes can contribute to our view of medicine.

Acknowledgments

My thanks to my outstanding colleagues in the MacArthur Foundation's Mind-Body Network for their personal example and for their highly stimulating dialogue, which has found its way into this volume in a number of places. I also thank Bob Rose, the Mind-Body Network's Director, for his generous support while I was doing the bulk of the writing.

I am especially grateful to those who commented on specific sections of this book and encouraged me to continue in this effort, including Mustafa al'Absi, Stephan Bongard, Michael Giordano, Tom Hall, Anne Harrington, John Sheridan, and Jay Weiss. I extend my most sincere gratitude to the editor of this series, J. Rick Turner, who was a constant source of encouragement and a superb judge of style and substance. Similarly I am most indebted to my colleague and former student Sue Everson, who provided very constructive criticism, greatly enhancing the value of several chapters.

Finally I must thank all my research collaborators who helped me develop much of the thought that went into this book; Loretta Sandlain, for her secretarial support; and Judy Silverstein, for her library research.

To my parents

Behavioral Medicine
and Biomedicine

In 1928, American physiologist Walter Cannon addressed the Massachusetts Medical Society on the subject of emotions and disease. He noted that

> a wife who was free from any cardiac disorder, saw her husband walking arm in arm with a strange woman and acting in such a way as to rouse jealousy and suspicion. Profoundly stirred by the incident the wife hastened home and remained there several days. She then began to fear going out lest she might meet her husband with her rival. After days of wretchedness she was persuaded by a friend to venture forth, "probably in a state of abject terror" . . . but she had not gone far when she ran back to her home. Then she noted that her heart was thumping hard, that she had a sense of oppression in her chest and a choking sensation. Later attempts to go outdoors produced the same alarming symptoms. She began to feel that she might die on the street if she went out. There was no organic disease of the heart, and yet slight effort as she moved from her home brought on acute distress. (Cannon, 1928, p. 169)

It is always impressive to see how the effect of a psychologically meaningful event can change a person's physical state. Examples like this lead one to ask how an idea can change the body.

This book is concerned with mental activity and behavioral processes and their relationships to states of health and disease. I specifically take up the question of psychological stress and describe how mental activity can produce negative effects on the body, perhaps leading to disease or even death. When I say *behavior*, I mean not only moving and talking but also thoughts and emotions. Ideas about the relationship between the mind and the body have been debated since the ancient Greeks. In fact, the *mind-body problem* is one of the fundamental philosophical and scientific issues in human knowledge. Combining our thinking about behavior and mental life into our thinking about medicine is essential to developing a truly behavioral medicine.

Although the example above is believable, we have little understanding of how this woman's seeing her husband with his girlfriend led to extreme fear and her physical symptoms. We have become increasingly familiar with the mechanisms of the brain and how these control the rest of the body. Similarly, psychology has increased our knowledge about how we learn, think, and take in the world. Still, studies of the workings of the body and the processes of the mind seem to exist in separate departments at universities and in separate compartments of our thinking. This division hinders our understanding of the woman patient and the relationships among her experiences, emotions, and physical state. In considering behavioral influences in health and disease, we need to have a way of thinking about how words can affect the body. We understand how bacteria and viruses can invade our body and how heart disease develops in the arteries of the heart, but we are not yet fully comfortable with the idea that psychological processes such as emotions and personality characteristics can influence these same disease processes.

To make sense of psychological stress and behavioral medicine, I begin with a brief mention of the development of modern Western medicine. I next sketch some new approaches to understanding behavioral interactions with health and disease. I then discuss a common basis for understanding physical and psychological stress reactions and move to an examination of disease processes as they may be affected by such stress-related processes. The final topic area is the differences between people in such stress-related processes. This book therefore is intended as a short review of how our behaviors, especially ideas and associated emotions, come to have power over our bodies. In the process, I hope the reader will gain some useful insights into how psychological theory can contribute to our view of medicine.

▓ The Age of Enlightenment and the Emergence of Scientific Thought

The reader's task is to understand the role of the brain in health and disease. Modern medicine—what I call *biomedicine*—represents one of the major successes of science. Our science is the product of the Western worldview. I will therefore examine our worldview and take note of the kind of science that emerged from that viewpoint. In the process, the reader may see how it is difficult for traditional Western biomedicine to provide treatment for patients like the woman in the above example.

Our present worldview can be thought of as dating from the 17th century, a period coming at the end of the renaissance and at the beginning of the age of enlightenment. But we did not suddenly invent our world in the 1600s: Ideas developed before that time continue to shape our worldview. We think of ourselves as modern persons who must surely see things differently than the Greeks did, but in fact we often embellish ancient concepts without replacing them.

The Greeks saw reality as having two fundamentally different aspects. There was the physical world, perceived through one's senses, and the world of ideas, the intelligible world of true knowledge. Reachable through reason alone, the unchangeable world of pure forms was the essence of the physical world. For Plato, the world had physical properties, but lurking behind these were essential, nonphysical properties. Plato explains, "One trait in the philosopher's character we can assume is his love of the knowledge that reveals eternal reality, the realm unaffected by change and decay" (Plato, ca. 380 B.C.E./1964, p. 274). Later, he notes that the visible world is changeable and illusory. For Plato, there are four ordered classes of reality. First there are shadows and reflections of things in the world as perceived through our senses. These are seen as subject to illusion and misinterpretation. Second comes true objects, which are somewhat more certain but still subject to the vagaries of our fallible senses. Third comes the sciences, which are more certain in their foundation than sensory experience. Fourth is the world of pure ideas, the world of true essences of physical objects.

Two very important themes emerge from this brief description of Greek thought. First, the Greeks placed great value on the power of human reason to understand nature—an idea that we also hold today. Second, the Greeks had a metaphysically dualistic view of the world. Every thing had its essential qualities and its physical qualities. The world of the mind was not of the physical world.

If we move ahead to the renaissance and the enlightenment, we can still see clearly the traces of this metaphysical dualism. At the beginning of the 17th century, the rational study of nature was becoming an important means to gain knowledge, but the emergence of science came into conflict with religious doctrine that dictated that true knowledge was handed down and not discovered. René Descartes, the 17th-century French philosopher and mathematician, made historic contributions to epistemology and mathematics; by the time of his death, all the main pieces of our modern worldview were in place. He provided the philosophical beginnings of modern science and medicine, but he left the Greek dualism in place to deal with the religious and political realities of his time.

Descartes and the Mechanical Model of Living Things

Descartes established the core principles of modern scientific epistemology, summarized in *Discourse on Method* (1637/1956). He answers the question, "How do we know that our knowledge is valid?" The adoption of a particular epistemology determines how we might go about acquiring knowledge, what sorts of theories about the world are legitimate.

In *Discourse,* Descartes (1637/1956) addresses the issue of how to study the natural world. He strongly rejects any reliance on external authority as a source of received knowledge. For Descartes, knowledge is valid only if based on careful observation informed by the use of reason. He emphasizes that the world can be seen as a series of objects interacting as a complex machine, much in the way that a clock can be seen as a series of interacting springs, wheels, gears, and levers. Also, like a clock, the world can be disassembled into simpler subunits so as to study the complex machine as a series of simpler subassemblies. Descartes then addresses the question of how to go about the study of living things. His position is that living things have a physical body that can be studied just like a clock, and, with effort, the body can be understood completely.

The problem for Descartes (1637/1956) in defining this epistemology is to address how living things, especially humans, seem different from other machines. Living things are spontaneous and, well, alive. Machines, on the other hand, just sit there and do not really do anything on their own. In addition, as living humans, we are aware of our thoughts and sensations, things surely denied to machines, even modern computers. Most important, the body is made of physical matter that eventually dies and disappears, whereas the soul is seen by Descartes and most contemporaries as nonphysical and immortal. This Greek-based view of human nature, inherited by Descartes, is reinforced by our subjective sense of ourselves as having a nonphysical mind inhabiting our physical bodies (Ryle, 1949). Finally, Descartes confronts the dominant power of his day, the Catholic Church, which held strongly to the Greek view of things and was prepared to punish anyone who taught a different view. For perhaps all these reasons, Descartes writes, "I then described the rational soul, and showed that it could not possibly be derived from the powers of matter . . . but must have been specially created" (p. 38). What Descartes means by the soul is very close to our view of the mind. Descartes manages to patch together a view of humans as biological machines inhabited by a nonmechanical soul that causes the machinery to move by acting through the pineal gland via microscopic tubes running to the nervous system.

Descartes (1637/1956) moved science ahead by establishing the idea that we could take a mechanistic view of living things, but he left us with a significant conceptual problem by reserving a special place for our minds, arguing that they were subject to different laws than our body. This *mind-body dualism* has hindered our unified understanding of the relationship between what we call our psychological or mental existence and our physical presence. The split view of ourselves that we inherit from Descartes is the source of the difficulty we have in understanding how ideas can influence the body or how one's mind can be an agent in health and disease.

The Worldview and Premises of Modern Science

When I talk about the view of the fundamental nature of reality, I am talking about *metaphysics*. Western metaphysics, based on Descartes, goes something like this:

First, there is a single, fundamental, material level of reality. All things are made of increasingly complex assemblages of ordinary matter. Thus, it follows that more complex levels of organization do not involve ontologically, or fundamentally, new entities beyond the more basic elements of which they are made up. Put another way, more complex machines are simply combinations of simpler machines. They never become something fundamentally different than machines, no matter how subtle and complex they are. It also follows that there is a unified, physicalist language in whose vocabulary all phenomena subject to scientific inquiry can in principle be described. That is, we do not need a different language or set of scientific concepts to describe increasingly complex machines, even when these are biological organisms.

The second metaphysical principle deriving from the Cartesian mechanical view is that the material world has an external permanency over which nonmaterial activities (e.g., mental or physical) can have no effect. To make this point, Descartes (1637/1956, p. 6) explicitly denounces the claims of those who say they can move through time and space and levitate objects as the falsehoods of charlatans and magicians.

Based on these metaphysical principles, science views the world in several specific ways. We can understand complex things by first studying their simpler parts (*reductionism*). The rules for such a study are derived from the same rules that explain mechanical objects (*mechanism*). Everything we observe has a physical cause (*causality*). Everything is therefore determined by some complex of causes (*determinism*). Last, we have inherited the unfortunate model of ourselves as things with two distinct natures, physical and spiritual (*dualism*). These points are discussed at length by Foss and Rothenberg (1988).

The Mind-Body Problem

Philosophers have noted the severe problems that arise when one holds to Descartes's (1637/1956) dualism. Ryle (1949) puts it best:

> There is a doctrine about the nature and place of minds . . . prevalent among theorists and even among laymen.
>   The official doctrine, which hails chiefly from Descartes, is something like this . . . every human being has both a body and a mind. Some would prefer to say that every human being is both a body and a mind. His body

and his mind are ordinarily harnessed together, but after the death of the body his mind may continue to exist and function.

Human bodies are in space and are subject to the mechanical laws which govern all other bodies in space.

But minds are not in space, nor are their operations subject to mechanical laws.

Such an outline is the official theory. I shall often speak of it, with deliberate abusiveness, as "the dogma of the Ghost in the Machine." (pp. 11-16)

The powerful dualistic position that Ryle (1949) ridicules put the emerging science of medicine into a physical framework from which the mind is largely excluded and, in the mainstream of medicine, diseases are seen only in physical (and nonmental) terms.

As powerful as Descartes's (1637/1956) position was, a minority of his contemporaries suspected that something was basically wrong with his mind-body dualism. The flaw was that Descartes made the basic mistake of seeing matter as inanimate, unmoving, and incapable of behaving on its own without being moved by some outside force (see Toulmin, 1967). Indeed, the inherent inertia of matter was the dominant view of Descartes's time, in line with Newton's mechanical model.

The minority view is best stated by Mettrie, who claimed in the 18th century that matter was not really unmoving stuff and that thought was not incompatible with the nature of matter (see Toulmin, 1967). In other words, Descartes's (1637/1956) mistake was in not recognizing that the ability to interact, or behave, is a fundamental property of matter. An important conclusion of Mettrie's is that living things do not have to be inhabited by mysterious mind stuff to be able to think and act spontaneously. Instead, thinking and acting are behavioral properties that stem from the physical composition of living things. At the time, Mettrie's position was a radical view and not widely shared. It contrasted too sharply with the commonsense folklore that physical matter is unmoving.

▧ Claude Bernard and the Modern Biomedical Model

In spite of Descartes's (1637/1956) strong views on the mechanical basis for the workings of the body, advances occurred mainly in the physical sciences.

Biology was left aside while physics and chemistry made rapid strides. Even in the mid-1800s, the workings of the body were considered by some to be impossible to study because of the invisible "vital forces" that occupied all living things. Claude Bernard (1865/1961) and other founders of modern physiology argue forcefully against this viewpoint. In line with Mettrie, Bernard insists that living things obey all the same laws as nonliving things. Even though living things appear to be self-moving and self-guided, this does not mean that they are inhabited by a nonphysical life force. The job of science is to learn to apply the laws of physics and chemistry to the new science of physiology.

Bernard's (1865/1961) great contribution to medicine was to extend the Cartesian epistemology to legitimize the study of living things as physical entities. The mechanistic model he promotes does not dispense with the dualism established by Descartes (1637/1956) 200 years earlier, however. Although the mysterious life forces are done away with in the organs and muscles, they remain present in the brain in the form of our mental processes. This leaves a system of medicine based on physical principles, but from which the mind is excluded. With minor exceptions, this is the dominant view in Western biomedicine. Although this viewpoint is gradually changing because of advances in the neurosciences and related biological and behavioral fields, this newer viewpoint is only beginning to be felt in scientific medicine.

Concepts of Wellness and Disease

Today's science of medicine also has a physical basis. Disease is a physical condition. Disease exists apart from the observer, and so the social organization or thoughts of the sick person have no effect on the disease. This view of disease as a physical process, and the continuing view that we have a nonphysical mind inside a machine-like body, has made it difficult to develop a behavioral medicine. In a truly behavioral medicine, behavior, including thoughts, feelings, and lifestyle, would occupy the same conceptual space as physical bodies. The mind-brain and the body influence each other, and our health and our behavior are part of the same process of life.

SUMMARY

As the early scientists banished occult (hidden) forces from mechanical bodies to make way for understanding their function, so the pioneer physiologists banished vital forces from the workings of the body to understand its physical workings.

Just as Descartes (1637/1956) makes an exception in his epistemology for the claimed unique nature of the soul, however, Bernard (1865/1961) and later physiologists make an exception for the role of the mind in influencing the body. The mind, therefore, remained a mysterious, nonphysical presence inside our biological machinery.

The discussion of stress in later chapters helps clarify the nature of the relationship between the mind and the body. Recent advances in biology and the neurosciences provides a clearer picture of the inherently interactive, behavioral character of neurons and neuronal systems. This understanding provides a basis for rethinking the relationship between the physical side of our nature and our mental existence.

FURTHER READING

Bernard, C. (1961). *An introduction to the study of experimental medicine* (H. C. Greene, Trans.). New York: Collier. (Originally published 1865)

Bernard's writings are historically significant and highly entertaining as an account of the emergence of modern physiology. His work stands as the basis of our contemporary understanding of the workings of the body at rest and during stress.

Toulmin, S. (1967). Neuroscience and human understanding. In G. C. Quarton, T. Melnechuk, & F. O. Schmitt (Eds.), *The neurosciences: A study program* (pp. 822-832). New York: Rockefeller University Press.

This is a rich, powerfully informative, and concise discussion of the relationship between the study of the brain and the emerging reconceptualization of consciousness. These topics are fundamental to our understanding of how the mind can influence the body.

Wozniak, R. H. (1992). *Mind and body: René Descartes to William James.* Bethesda, MD: National Library of Medicine.

Wozniak provides a thorough historical commentary on the major lines of thought related to this paradox during the development of modern psychology.

Psychosocial Models
of Health and Disease

Most people know, or at least most believe, that we cannot use our minds directly to influence outside objects. We cannot levitate things. We cannot transport ourselves by means of thought. And yet the example in Chapter 1 reminds us that the mind influences the body, sometimes in dramatic ways. How can we change the state of our body by our state of mind? This is the central question of this book. Later chapters concentrate on how the mind can create the conditions for bodily stress responses. Before I discuss psychological stress, I will consider how mental processes can affect the health of the body, interacting with disease processes. This brief consideration will allow me to place the topic of psychological stress into a behavioral medicine framework.

I said in Chapter 1 that our metaphysical case of split personality leaves us few conceptual tools to help us understand and explain how the mind alters the body. As a result, our system of medicine has not readily adopted a scientifically grounded model in which thoughts and emotions affect health.

I will start by analyzing the infectious disease process using a very restricted biomedical model. I will show how this model can be usefully expanded to include the behaviors of the patient. In a second example, I will describe how a behavioral medicine can be useful in coming to understand the way in which placebo effects operate. Finally, I will consider how a behavioral medicine approach is especially helpful in conceptualizing cause and treatment in complex diseases such as coronary artery disease.

The key concepts in this chapter are

1. Disease processes should be seen as dynamic interactions between the causative agent and the affected organism.
2. The disease and its treatment are embedded in a hierarchy of systemic controls—that is, lower levels of the system are in two-way interaction with higher levels in the system and each level integrates and regulates the levels below it. This point is discussed in more detail in Chapter 4, where I describe the autonomic nervous system and higher controls in the brainstem and hypothalamus.
3. The hierarchy of causal influences ultimately includes complex behaviors such as the thoughts and emotions of the affected person and the sociocul- turally determined environment in which that person lives.

▧ The Standard Biomedical Model and New Approaches to Medicine

In line with the Cartesian idea, the standard biomedical model goes like this: Disease is a linearly causal process, "a condition of the living animal or plant body or of one of its parts that impairs the performance of a vital function" (*Webster's Ninth New Collegiate Dictionary*, 1988). Disease is a disorder of an otherwise smooth running machine. The cure is to disrupt the causative agent at the physical level to help the machine repair itself and regain normal function. In the extreme form of this model, following Western scientific tradition, the workings of the mind are not relevant to the disease or its cure.

Figure 2.1 is a conceptual diagram of this form of the biomedical model. The diagram illustrates a normally functioning person being acted on by some pathogenic stimulus such as an infection, a cancer, or coronary heart disease. The mode of therapy is a direct physical intervention to restore the person's healthy, well-ordered state. Such therapies may include the administration of an antibiotic to cure a bacterial infection, the application of chemotherapy for a cancer, or coronary bypass grafts for coronary heart disease. All these treatments have known restorative, if not curative, properties. Their application in individual cases results in one of the three outcomes on the right of Figure 2.1. The hope is that the patient gets better. Other outcomes also occur, however, including continued illness or death.

A key feature of this model is that the cure works with or without the knowledge or assistance of the patient. The cure is purely physical and not affected by the thoughts or emotional state of the person being treated. This traditional model has the following characteristics:

1. The model has one-way causation. The pathogen acts on the host and not the other way around.
2. The disease is a physiological process, and treatment operates on the disease state at that level.
3. Therefore, the model is nonhierarchical, meaning that different levels of complexity in the system, particularly higher nervous system controls related to thoughts and emotions, do not interact with each other.
4. As a result, the model is dualistic. The mental status of the person is incidental to the cause of the disease and its cure.

This description of the traditional biomedical model is presented in stark terms to contrast it clearly with the potential contributions of a behavioral medicine. Practicing physicians are aware of the power of thoughts and emotions to affect health, however. The problem for the individual physician is that the standard model has no conceptual framework for integrating this knowledge into practice or for turning these relationships to its advantage. Knowing that the mental state of the patient may affect the disease and response to treatment therefore becomes part of the art, rather than the science, of medicine.

In considering the contrasting features of the biomedical model and the behavioral medicine model presented here, the following points should be kept in mind.

1. The traditional biomedical model has proven to be very effective at treating disease. When I speak of the shortcomings of the model, I mean that it is limited because it has no way to incorporate the knowledge that thoughts and emotions can enhance development of diseases or promote their cures.

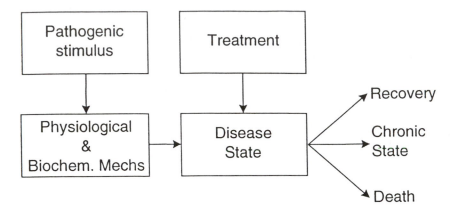

Figure 2.1. Traditional medical model of the disease process. The disease process and the treatment are shown acting on a passive organism, and the treatment and disease do not interact. This depicts a restrictive view of the traditional medical model.

2. Although the potential power of thoughts and emotions in the processes of health and disease are known, these psychological processes are rarely, if ever, the sole cause of disease. Instead, such mental processes can alter the body in ways that may aggravate, or alleviate, otherwise existing disease processes.

3. We are only just beginning to understand how interactions between psychological processes and disease pathophysiology may occur. The information in this chapter is primarily a formal description of how such interactions may operate. Later chapters deal with these interactions in a more mechanistic fashion.

4. The possibility that behavioral influences may alter disease processes and the mechanisms involved must be approached with the same degree of scientific caution used in understanding disease and cure within the standard biomedical model.

When I refer to the virtues of a behavioral medicine, I am aware that this emerging framework has potential to help in the mind-body integration in medicine, but the promise has yet to be fully realized. There is a great deal of work to be done.

▓ A Biobehavioral Model of Disease and Treatment

The model of disease outlined in the previous section is narrow. It restricts the view of the range of processes acting on our bodies, and this limits thoughts about the causes and therapeutic interventions possible in a behavioral medicine. The view of the disease process can be expanded by embedding the first model in one that includes the person's learning history and sociocultural environment, as shown in Figure 2.2.

This enlarged model of disease and treatment shows three important interactions between the person and the environment.

1. The person's psychosocial processes, meaning his or her thoughts, emotions, and spoken words, interact with the social and cultural environments—these informational interchanges, for example, information concerning the nature of the disease and its cure, can affect its outcome.
2. Not only does the pathogen affect the person's physiology, but the actions of the immune system also alter the pathogen. This interaction is also primarily exchange of information between host and pathogen.
3. The treatment still acts to alter the disease state, as it did in the first example. I have included interactions among the treatment, pathogen, and host and the social environment and psychosocial functioning as processes that affect treatment outcome, however.

Pathogen-Host Interactions

To illustrate the informational and behavioral elements incorporated into Figure 2.2, think about pathogen-host interactions based on current knowledge in immunology. In this framework, the pathogen provides information about itself to the host. This signals the immune system that a foreign organism is present, that the organism has certain proteins on its outer membrane, and as to how to recognize these proteins. The immune system then seeks the foreign cells and attacks them with one or more defenses. In turn, the invader may have evolved counterdefenses to evade or trick the immune cells, allowing them to survive longer in the host.

The pathogen-immune interaction illustrates how a wide range of behaviors, in this case at the cellular level, may play a role in the processes of disease and treatment. First, the host is involved in a dynamic, interactive

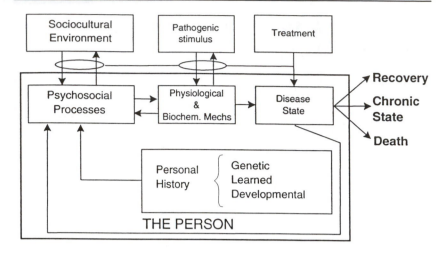

Figure 2.2. Expanded model of the disease process. The disease process interacts with the person, and psychological processes interact with physiological processes. In turn, the person interacts with the sociocultural environment. The treatment, disease, and environment are all capable of interacting as well.

relationship with the pathogen. Second, this interaction is characterized by the exchange of information about the nature of the invader and the form of the host's defensive response. Third, the virulence of the infection is the outcome of the interaction between the host and the pathogen.

These interactions, exchanges of information, and virulence of the disease are behavioral interchanges. Although we normally think of behaviors as the overt actions of ourselves and others, the term *behavior* should also include inner thoughts and feelings. The idea that cellular interactions also have the characteristics of behaviors should not be disturbing, because behavior is a good description of the interactive sequence of invasion, identification, cellular attack, and counterattack involved in the infectious disease process. This expanded use of the term readily allows one to incorporate the basic disease mechanism into a larger model encompassing psychosocial and sociocultural processes, as Figure 2.2 does. As you will see in Chapter 8, the dynamic properties of immune system behavior also provide abundant pathways for the study of interactions with higher nervous processes, such as emotions. For this reason, I have emphasized at several points the importance of seeing the disease and treatment as an event that occurs in a hierarchically integrated system and not as an event isolated at the cellular or organ level.

Psychosocial-Sociocultural Interactions

Considering sociocultural processes, it is not hard to imagine how the course and outcome of invasion by a pathogen will surely be different for a person whose learning history includes the knowledge of antibiotics or for one whose sociocultural background calls for a treatment such as prayer but not going to a physician. Knowledge of disease and choices of treatment are fundamentally informational and behavioral processes, just as the interaction between host and invader are informational and behavioral interactions at the cellular level. These learned and culturally conditioned information exchanges and behaviors determine the course and outcome of the disease, as do the interactions at the immune system level.

Another important feature of the expanded view of disease is that the model is not linearly causal. It is recursive and interactive. In Figure 2.1, the arrows point in one direction, suggesting that the causal events work in only one direction. In Figure 2.2, the two-way arrows invite one to think about the course of the disease and its treatment as repeated, or recursive, interactions. Disease and treatment become behavioral processes unfolding over time as an ongoing interchange between host and pathogen.

This model implies that treatment of an infectious disorder could have significant psychological, behavioral, and cultural elements. By considering such a model of disease, one can begin to see that the physical aspects of the disease and the psychosocial and cultural processes are no longer clearly different. Note that I have included two-way arrows between psychosocial processes and physiological processes. I am acknowledging that thoughts and emotions are intimately connected to the workings of the body. A clearer discussion of the mechanisms involved is provided in Chapters 5 through 9. In a model such as this, the concepts of *somatic* disease, *psychosomatic* disease, or *psychological* disease are no longer categorically different terms. They merely call attention to different facets of the same process. In this sense, the story told at the beginning of Chapter 1 and the dualistic sense of mind and body that my initial question implied begin to look fuzzy. Some additional examples should break down the distinction further. The view of treatment, and even prevention, changes when one takes such an expanded view of disease.

▓ Placebo Effects

For the second example, I will discuss placebo effects. In using a placebo, the patient takes a preparation that has no known biological activity, and yet the patient responds and perhaps improves. This is a *placebo effect* from the Latin phrase for "I shall please." This implies that the medical effect has to do with a mental process associated with thoughts and emotions. In fact, the patient has to think that he or she is taking medicine to cure a specific disease. To understand placebo effects, one must examine information processes, including the beliefs and cultural norms of the patient and physician. When one considers the dynamics of placebo effects, one realizes that all the interactions outlined in Figure 2.2 may accompany any form of treatment. That is, every form of treatment, placebo or otherwise, can have elements of psychological causation at work. This topic is discussed at length in Benson and McCallie (1979) and Kirsch (1990).

Current thinking is that placebos operate because of the expectancies of the person receiving them. Expectancies, in turn, develop in a certain sociocultural environment and in persons with a certain learning history. We learn to expect things about the world from our culture and from our own experience. A patient taking pills in a drug study who is unknowingly assigned to the placebo control group may say explicitly or implicitly, "Doctors give people medicines that make them well. The pills I'm taking are designed to cure my illness. I have taken pills in the past that cured me of other illnesses, and perhaps these will work as well." These words describe expectations about what the pills might be able to do. In some cases, these ideas result in outright cures or therapeutic effects as large as those caused by the active drug, as discussed by Benson and McCallie (1979). For example, in various studies of medications for coronary heart disease, 33-37% of patients given placebos improved subjectively and objectively for up to a year or more— impressive results for an inactive compound.

This kind of outcome does not fit a traditional physicalist model of medicine. Placebo effects can only be understood as being mediated informationally by the central nervous system. Figure 2.3 illustrates that the traditional model of disease does not have a mechanism that permits physiologically inactive substances to have a measurable effect on the patient. There is no direct means by which the substance can intervene in the disease process.

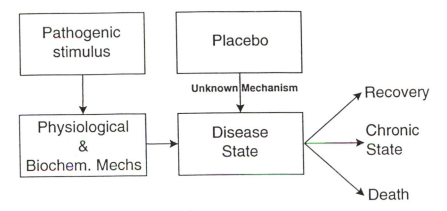

Figure 2.3. Placebo effects in the context of a traditional medical model. In a medical model that ignores psychological processes, there are no adequate mechanisms to explain the operation of a placebo.

This is not to say that traditional medicine ignores placebos, only that it has no metaphysical and epistemological basis for understanding them. This uneasy recognition that something occurs but that we have no means for conceptualizing or controlling the phenomenon is uncomfortable, and it illustrates in another way the sort of problem we have inherited along with our dualistic metaphysics. An expanded model, such as the one in Figure 2.2, is more inclusive and opens up possibilities for incorporating placebo effects into our thinking. One can now begin to consider how experience, beliefs, and cultural norms might set the stage for physical changes to occur following ingestion of an otherwise inert substance in a treatment context.

Psychoneuroimmunology

In considering placebo effects, I should briefly mention important recent developments in our understanding of how psychological events may alter the functions of the immune system. Ader and his colleagues (Ader & Cohen, 1993) performed ingenious experiments to study how conditioned stimuli can alter immune function. In a prototype experiment, a group of rats was given a drug known to suppress the function of the immune system. Simultaneous with the drug, saccharine was given in the animals' water. At a later time, after the function of the immune system had recovered, the

animals were again exposed to the saccharine water, but without the immunosuppressive drug. This resulted in a resuppression of immune function. It
so happens that to a rat, saccharine tastes different from sugar, and so
saccharine provided a novel taste sensation for these animals. Novel tastes
are very salient stimuli for rats.

Ader and his coworkers (Ader & Cohen, 1993) suggest that this phenomenon of saccharine-induced immunosuppression could be accounted for
by a process of classical conditioning. In classical conditioning, a stimulus
that has automatic effects on the body (such as food, which will lead to
salivation in a dog) and a stimulus unconnected with the original response
(such as a bell or tone) are presented. Eventually, the bell comes to elicit
salivation, and so the salivation has become conditioned to the sound. In
Ader's studies, one can think of the immunosuppressive drug as an unconditional stimulus (US), one that automatically produces an unconditional
immunosuppressive response (UR) due to its direct action on the system. One
can also think of the saccharine as a conditional stimulus (CS), one that has
no such effect on its own. Finally, one can see how the response to the
saccharine alone became a conditioned response (CR) developed from the
original UR associated with the CS-US pairing.

I use this brief example to note that personal experience exemplified by
conditioning may change the functioning of the immune system, among
others. In fact, one can think of the saccharine in Ader's (Ader & Cohen,
1993) studies as a kind of placebo that acquired its effect through conditioning. Finally, note that the taste of saccharine to the rat is really an
informational stimulus. It has no power of its own, but it becomes a piece of
information, a symbol, that something else may also happen, such as the
administration of the immunosuppressive drug. In this way one can begin to
think about how ideas—symbols—may come to have power over our bodies.

▓ Cultural, Intrapersonal, and Physiological Influences in Coronary Heart Disease

As a last example, consider what happens in the diagnosis and treatment of
a complex, chronic disease such as coronary heart disease. This example
provides even richer sources of behavioral input to the disease process and
its alleviation than in the case of infectious disease. Coronary heart disease,
or coronary artery disease, is the result of the gradual accumulation of

cholesterol-rich fatty plaques and thickened areas in the walls of the blood vessels that supply blood to the heart. This ultimately leads to an attenuated blood supply to the continually working heart muscle. The muscle receives too little oxygen, often causing the oppressive chest pain of angina pectoris. Occasionally, a blood clot may form at the site of a thickened atherosclerotic lesion, completely blocking blood flow to the heart muscle downstream, resulting in a heart attack, referred to by cardiologists as a myocardial infarction, or just an MI.

Current treatments for this disease involve bypass grafts that circumvent the lesioned areas of coronary artery by attaching new vessels borrowed from other parts of the body; balloon angioplasty, which expands the narrowed areas of vessel by inserting a tiny balloon at the end of a catheter and inflating it at the restricted segment; or putting the patient on a low cholesterol diet, sometimes supplemented by cholesterol-lowering drugs. Coronary artery bypass grafts were the most common major surgical procedure performed in the United States in 1992. All these treatments are strictly within the traditional framework—they intervene in the pathogenic process at the tissue level.

The top of Figure 2.4 shows a restricted, physicalist view of coronary artery disease and its treatment. In this view, the cause is a diet too high in cholesterol and saturated fats, perhaps helped along by a genetic predisposition to atherosclerosis. The cure is some combination of the therapies above. More recent evidence, however, suggests that personal behaviors and cultural practices have much to do with the development of coronary heart disease. The United States has a cultural practice of eating a diet high in animal fat and total calories. Furthermore, some persons may aggravate the development of heart disease by regularly engaging in vigorous competitive behaviors accompanied by a hostile attitude. This constellation of extreme activity and hostile emotions, known as *Type A behavior,* may be associated with frequent elevations of blood pressure along with stress hormone secretion and the release of stored fat molecules into the bloodstream. These physiological processes may accelerate lesion formation and growth.

With an expanded view of the disorder, depicted in the bottom of Figure 2.4, one can see the interplay of sociocultural, genetic, and personal habits in the etiology of the disease. The expanded model allows the consideration that coronary heart disease does not have a simple unitary cause. Instead, a genetic heritage in combination with a constellation of overt behaviors and emotional predispositions occurring in a certain cultural environment all act

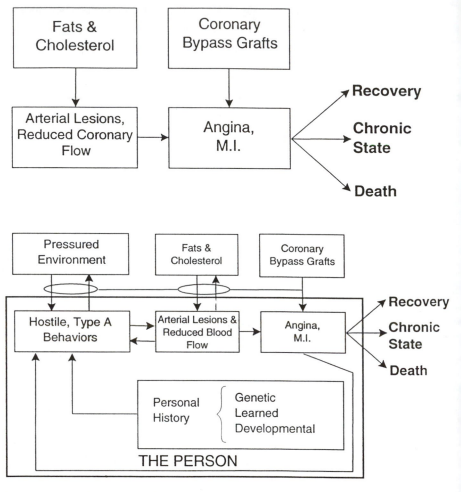

Figure 2.4. Traditional model of coronary artery disease (top) and an expanded model (bottom). Treatments for coronary disease are shown as addressing the acute effects of the illness without addressing behavioral sources of the disorder.

to increase or decrease disease risk. Furthermore, this expanded disease model not only allows for a more thorough view of the development of coronary heart disease, but it begins to provide insights into possible modes of therapy not possible under the more restricted model in the top of Figure 2.4. For example, it may be possible to provide cognitive and behavioral training to persons subject to frequent, intense hostile interactions, thus lessening the destructive effects of blood pressure and catecholamine rises on the atherosclerotic vessels. In fact, such treatment in men who had experienced a first heart attack resulted in a significantly lower rate of second attacks compared to men who received only standard care (Friedman et al., 1986).

We inherited a dualistic view of ourselves via the Cartesian tradition. This leaves us with the problem of how psychosocial and sociocultural processes, which appear to be nonphysical, can act as causes of disease or as modes of treatment.

▧ Psychosocial Theories of Disease and Treatment

To understand all the causes of disease and to consider the greatest possible range of treatments, one should recognize that neither the causes nor the cures are adequately described by a simple linear model. An expanded definition of disease might look like this: a disorder of body functions or systems arising from malfunction at the level of physiological, psychophysiological, or sociocultural functioning.

The expanded biobehavioral model of disease not only helps us think about causes, it also provides insights into elements critical to treatment. Several authors have considered the role of psychological and sociocultural processes in treatment (e.g., Elstein & Bordage, 1979). We may consider a revised view of treatment, taking into account some traditional and nontraditional questions:

1. Who is being treated? The patient's psychological composition, learning history, and cultural background may be important elements in developing a plan of treatment.
2. What is the specific disease state? Accurate diagnosis is crucial to successful treatment.
3. What factors limit treatment alternatives? Not all treatments are feasible at all times.
4. What is the social environment? This may facilitate some treatments and limit the uses of others.
5. What is the specific form of treatment? Clearly, all other considerations aside, the treatment must ultimately interact appropriately with the disease process at a physical level.

6. What is the therapist's psychological composition? The success of treatment may be influenced by the attitudes of the practitioner.

7. What is the mode of therapy? The form of therapy must be tailored to meet the restrictions imposed by the above.

8. What is the goal of treatment? Given any disease state, the goals of treatment will be based on realistic considerations of the above.

■ The Foundation of Behavioral Medicine

Behavioral medicine involves the study of how sociocultural and mind-brain processes can influence the health of an individual.

Schwartz (1979) argues that general systems theory offers a way to conceptualize the role of the mind-brain in health and disease. *Systems theory* describes how simple and complex systems are regulated and how they maintain that regulation when threatened with disruption. From the systems theory perspective, Schwartz points out that the brain is engaged constantly in hierarchically integrating information to regulate bodily functions, such as respiration. By hierarchical, he means that bodily functions have several layers of control, each layer being modified by the one above. The layered control concept provides a way of thinking about how our higher brain activities such as thoughts and emotions can act on lower centers to alter bodily functions. In calling the brain a health care system, Schwartz acknowledges that the brain ultimately plays the topmost role in regulating physiological systems. Finally, the brain is capable of interpreting and assimilating social and cultural information and reflecting these influences on the workings of the body.

Schwartz (1979) proposes a five-stage model to illustrate these processes:

1. The organism and the environment are involved in a two-way dialogue. We receive information from our external environment and continuously modify that environment by our actions.

2. The mind-brain integrates information from the external and internal environments and makes use of these two sources of information to determine regulation of the somatic organs.

3. The somatic organs alter their function according to activity determined by the brain. They also behave in ways that affect the internal environment.

4. In carrying out its regulatory role, the brain makes heavy use of *interoceptive* information. For example, in the short-term regulation of blood pressure, the brainstem receives constant input from the baroreceptors located in the

aorta and carotid arteries. Deviations from normal pressure lead to rapid changes in the heart's rate and force of contraction. This allows sudden pressure changes to be compensated for almost instantly. These processes happen automatically and out of our awareness.

5. Finally, it is possible for the brain to use external sources of information to regulate the body. The most striking example of such regulation is biofeedback. In biofeedback, a bodily function normally not accessible to awareness, such as blood pressure, is displayed visually or auditorally to allow conscious access to the momentary state of the pressure. By this means, it becomes possible with practice to raise or lower pressure for short periods by altering processes controlling pressure, such as heart rate. Biofeedback therefore provides another information channel for the brain to have access to and alter processes in the body.

In considering Schwartz's (1979) ideas on the regulation of body processes by the brain and the expanded disease model described in Figure 2.2, one can see that both place a significant emphasis on the role of information received by the brain to alter the functions of the body. Schwartz makes the important point that there is no fundamental difference in the interoceptive information the brain uses in its normal regulation of the body or in the information it receives from outside as determined by the behaviors of the individual or by the cultural environment. I return to the concept of hierarchical control by the brain in considering autonomic regulation in Chapter 4 and in my description of central nervous integration of psychological stress responses in Chapter 6.

SUMMARY

In this chapter, I described how the mind-body dualism of Descartes affected the Western view of physiology and medicine. In turn, this has led to an unnecessarily narrow view of the disease and treatment. I described a revised model of disease in which thoughts and emotions can be major elements in treatment. By acknowledging the role of psychosocial and sociocultural processes, behavioral medicine expands our ways of thinking about the influences on health and disease.

To bring this abstract discussion of behavioral medicine closer to reality, one needs to do two things. First, confront the obstacles to our thinking that are conditioned by our intellectual heritage. For this reason, I have sketched the history of our dualistic model of ourselves. If we continue to think of physical processes and mental or psychological functions as being in separate realms, then we will have a much more difficult time envisioning how our state of health and disease is conditioned by our thoughts, feelings, and actions. I will return to this topic in Chapter 10 and consider some ways of further dispelling the gaps in understanding. Second, address the mechanisms by which the brain controls our bodies and find the linkages between ideas and regulatory processes. We need to follow the steps between the idea and the bodily function if we are to answer the primary question of how an idea can come to have power over our bodies—how mental stress can affect health.

FURTHER READING

Foss, L., & Rothenberg, K. (1988). *The second medical revolution.* Boston: Shambhala.

Schwartz, G. (1979). The brain as a health care system. In G. C. Stone, F. Cohen, & N. E. Adler (Eds.), *Health psychology—A handbook* (pp. 549-571). San Francisco: Jossey-Bass.

These two primary sources for material covered in this chapter provide a broad view of the relationship of behavioral medicine to traditional medicine.

History of the
Concept of Stress

▦

▦ ▦ The first two chapters addressed the question of how ideas could alter
▦ ▦ the workings of the body. To approach this question, I began to make
a case for considering the role of the brain in altering physiological function
for better or worse. My argument can be summarized as follows: The brain
is how we make contact with the external environment. The interactions
are usually regulatory in nature and preserve normal, healthy functioning.
These transactions take place in a hierarchy of systems both up and down
the ladder.

The remainder of this book is concerned with mental stress's potential
for detrimental effects on the workings of the body. I consider the possibility
that dysregulation associated with stress may impair the health of the person.
Therefore, I address the question of stress responses as modifiers of health
within a behavioral medicine framework. This set of topics constitutes one
of the most challenging areas within which to examine the role of the mind
in health and disease.

■ Definition of Stress

Before going on, I should define the term *stress*. By stress, I mean a bodily or mental tension resulting from factors that tend to alter an existent equilibrium (*Webster's Ninth New Collegiate Dictionary*, 1988). For example, severe cold stresses our bodies if we are outside without proper clothing. A *stressor* is the thing that challenges the integrity, or health, of the body (*Webster's Ninth New Collegiate Dictionary*, 1988). A *stress response* is the compensatory reaction the body makes to the disturbance caused by the stressor.

One also can distinguish between physical and psychological stress. I refer to *physical stressors* as events having a direct physical threat value to one's well-being. Cold, in the above example, is clearly a physical stressor. There are others, such as heat, infection, or toxic substances. I also refer to *psychological stressors*. These events are challenges to our well-being, not because they are physically threatening but because of how we perceive them. We may find that a major personal disappointment or the sound of footsteps on a dark street in a strange neighborhood are very distressing and may evoke strong physical responses. The disappointment may evoke sadness, a heaviness in the chest, and feelings of lethargy. The footsteps may result in a sudden fear response accompanied by a racing heart and rapid breathing. It is important to note here that these physiological responses start out with events, psychological stressors, that are not physically threatening. The physiological responses and accompanying emotions arise because our disappointments or the footsteps behind us are challenges to our expectations about ourselves and the world or because they signal the potential of impending physical danger.

The end of this chapter includes some further comments about stressors and our responses to them. In later chapters, I will start out talking about physical stressors and responses to them and then move to the issue of psychological stress. In doing so, I will consider the question of ideas and how they can affect the body.

To begin the discussion of stress, it seems worthwhile to review a historical perspective on the development of the idea. This historical development places us squarely at the crux of the Cartesian dilemma and helps pose the questions necessary to keep these problematic issues clearly in focus.

▓ Claude Bernard and
the Vitalists

Certain ideas have a hold on the imagination in that they appear again and again in different forms. It has been this way with the idea that living things are special and have a privileged status in the material world. I noted before that Descartes's (1637/1956) ideas had a profound influence in helping the development of an empirical science of living things, even though he reserved a special place for the soul in the workings of the brain. But on the physical side, he thought that living things are material in nature and can be studied as one might study nonliving things.

In the early part of the 19th century, however, the school of vitalism reopened this issue by arguing that living things have special status in the order of things. *Vitalism* is the idea that living things are driven by nonphysical life forces and that these vital forces do not obey physicochemical laws. The vitalists held that living things are unique because they are suffused by the vital force. This made it impossible to study living organisms by a reductionistic strategy because a study of the subcomponents would disrupt the vital force, leaving the results of such study invalid.

An opposing viewpoint was taken by Bernard (1865/1961), a physiologist who argued that living things are amenable to a reductionistic research strategy. He uses the analogy of studying a steam engine. He notes that to an unsophisticated observer, a steam train would appear to have an internal force allowing the train to move itself. In the absence of the ability to study the components of such a machine, especially to examine how it makes use of energy to produce steam and to convert the pressure of the steam to mechanical forces propelling the wheels, it would be easy to conclude that such machines possess a mysterious internal force responsible for their movements. Descartes (1637/1956) uses similar mechanical analogies. It would have been obvious to any mid-19th-century observer, however, that a steam engine is in fact a machine whose actions are completely determined by the laws of mechanics. Bernard argues that the mechanical determinism associated with living things is in principle no different from that of the steam engine.

To support his position, Bernard (1865/1961) talks about the ways in which very simple organisms survive. He shows that very simple, one-celled organisms are dependent on a supportive external environment. These primitive creatures are able to maintain themselves only if the correct external factors such as moisture, temperature, oxygenation, and nutrients are available from the medium in which they live. Such animals are not capable of maintaining themselves independent of their external environments. The functions of such simple organisms clearly result from chemical and physical interactions with their surroundings, and they are highly responsive to any changes in external conditions. As a result of this dependency, the causal factors related to the maintenance of life are most obvious in these simple creatures, and the deterministic mechanisms by which life is maintained are therefore most easily seen.

In contrast, more highly developed organisms have a greater degree of autonomy from their environments. Mammals, for example, have an internal circulation that duplicates the conditions of the external medium surrounding one-celled life forms. They are capable of regulating temperature, acid-base balance of the blood, oxygenation of the cells, and a supply of nutrients by regulating the conditions of their blood supplies in the face of changing external conditions. For this reason, these complex life forms have the outward appearance of being autonomous and of possessing a hidden life force. The appearance of such a life force is really an illusion, however. In fact, complex animals are no less deterministically dependent on the conditions of the environment. At the cellular level, they are highly responsive to any change in the conditions of the internal environment. Therefore, Bernard (1865/1961) holds that the functions of complex living organisms are determined by both the external environment and the internal environment. He notes that the maintenance of life is critically dependent on keeping the internal environment constant in the face of a changing external environment. His key idea is that physical challenges to the integrity of an organism provoke responses to counteract those threats. This is the foundation of the modern concept of stress.

▓ Walter Cannon

The next major figure in the development of present ideas about stress and the regulation of physiological processes is Walter Cannon, the first professor of physiology at Harvard University. Cannon's research was concerned with the specific mechanisms of response to changes in the external environment while allowing for optimum bodily function (Cannon, 1929). He begins with Bernard's (1865/1961) idea that we are immersed in an internal fluid environment and have evolved mechanisms to keep this environment constant to support our cells. Cannon terms the process of maintaining this internal stability in the face of environmental change *homeostasis*. He notes that we have specialized sensory nerves to communicate the state of the rest of the body to the brain. The brain is able to detect nonoptimal internal states and it can call a variety of mechanisms into play to compensate correctly. We can respond to deviations from normal by invoking behavioral changes to alter the environment or by using autonomic and endocrine mechanisms to alter metabolic and other bodily processes to reachieve optimal conditions. He understands clearly that failure to meet such challenges to the homeostasis of the body could result in tissue damage or death if not countered by adequate responses to return the internal environment to normal.

Cannon's work was not confined to the mechanisms of physical challenges. He also concerned himself with the effect on the person of psychologically meaningful stimuli (1935), as seen in the example in Chapter 1.

Bernard (1865/1961) and Cannon (1929, 1935) contributed greatly to the philosophy of medical science and to the development of the concept of stress. Bernard's recognition that the cells of our bodies are in contact with an internal environment that has to be held constant led to the further recognition that there has to be a hierarchy of control mechanisms to compensate for changes from normal. I noted in Chapter 2 that to account fully for the ways in which persons maintain health, we have to develop a model in which successive layers of control are capable of managing the system during states of disease. Cannon studied the physical mechanisms we use to maintain homeostasis, but he also believed that loss of good health could result from dysregulation of the system at the level of psychological and sociocultural functioning.

My approach to behavioral medicine therefore begins with the physiological mechanisms by which environmental alterations are countered to maintain life; I will later examine the parallel effects of psychological challenges to well-being and how these too result in regulatory changes to meet these perceived threats.

▓ Hans Selye

The final figure in this history of stress is Hans Selye. He became the first to invoke the concept of stress systematically as a means to understand physiological regulatory responses to threats to the organism. He uses the term *stress* to represent the effects of any agent that seriously threatens the homeostasis of the organism, although I will more frequently use the term *stress response.* Selye calls agents causing stress responses *stressors,* just as I will.

Selye (1956) became interested in how animals are able to resist the effects of various challenges to their homeostasis, such as heat, cold, infection, and toxic substances. He observes that certain reactions always occur, including a decrease in the size of the thymus gland and other immune system organs, ulcers in the gastrointestinal tract, and enlargement of the adrenal glands. Because application of severe stressors always produces this set of changes, Selye argues that a core stress response could be evoked by many stressors, as well as specific responses called into play to meet the challenges unique to each type of stressor. The stress response, although severe in its manifestations, is recognized as necessary for survival and hence adaptive. Furthermore, repeated exposure to moderate stressors, Selye recognizes, could increase the ability of the organism to withstand more prolonged and severe exposure. Coaches make use of this idea by using frequent, moderate episodes of physical training to expand athletes' capacities to exercise harder and for longer periods in preparation for competition.

Although stress responses are part of the adaptive processes of the organism, Selye (1956) recognizes that severe, prolonged stress responses can also result in tissue damage and disease. This idea drew considerable attention to the potential harm caused by constant alterations in normal physiological function and forms the basis for current thinking that life stress can result in disease. It also draws attention to the importance of considering the stress response as a kind of balancing act in which too much or too little stress both carry undesirable consequences.

▓ Additional Considerations
About the Stress Concept

When one considers the historical discussion above, one can begin to see how all living things need to have mechanisms of regulation to keep their internal environments within limits to resist their destruction by outside forces. Thinking in this very general way, one might make several observations about stressors and stress responses and about living things in general.

I said above that stress is any source of disruption in the orderly workings of the body. I might rephrase that to say that a *stressor* is any challenge or threat to the normal processes or integrated function of a living thing. The response of the organism to that threat is the *stress response*. A threat exists when the environment begins to move beyond the range of normal for the system or the organism. So a small change in temperature in the living room is not a stressor. We have compensatory mechanisms to deal with that, and they are readily effective; but being locked out of the house on an evening when the temperature is below freezing might evoke not only severe physiological adjustments but major behavioral ones as well, including breaking into the house by any means necessary.

All biological systems are organized, interacting entities. Their functions are literally a form of systemic behavior. All such systems are able to tolerate a range of environmental conditions, and they must compensate for internal changes due to exposure to increasingly severe environmental conditions. At some point, very severe environmental circumstances will result in complete cessation of systems-level function (death). Stress implies a level of challenge that is severe enough to require major readjustments to meet the challenge or that is prolonged enough to alter system function.

Adjustments can occur at several levels: cells, organs, systems, higher levels of integration. When one level in the system is no longer able to compensate fully or adequately with the environmental challenge, higher-level controls come into play. Ultimately, these higher-level controls might include becoming aware that a problem exists, evaluating the problem, considering courses of action, and making behavioral adjustments to compensate for the imbalance. To return to the example of exposure to the cold, one can think of mild shivering as a systems response to a slightly cool living room and breaking in to the house as a severe behavioral adjustment, both of which have the ultimate purpose of returning the body temperature to normal.

Finally, bear in mind that people differ in how responsive they are to environmental threats and how they compensate. This issue of individual differences arises in Chapter 9 in the discussion of stress and disease predisposition.

SUMMARY

Our current ideas about stress and its effects are based on the idea that the machinery of the body has to have a way to protect itself when outside conditions change undesirably. Multiple control systems operate to maintain homeostasis. These homeostatic mechanisms are adaptive and serve to maintain life. They may also be damaging in themselves, however, during very severe or very prolonged states of stress. In Chapter 4, I begin to talk about the specific control mechanisms the body uses to maintain homeostasis.

FURTHER READING

Bernard, C. (1961). *An introduction to the study of experimental medicine* (H. C. Greene, Trans.). New York: Collier. (Original work published 1865)

A highly readable and interesting discussion of the early concepts in the field of physiology with emphasis on the epistemological groundwork that determined the development of biology from that time to the present.

Cannon, W. B. (1929). *Bodily changes in pain, hunger, fear, and rage* (2nd ed.). New York: Appleton.

Cannon's most important work, this book surprises the reader with its sophistication and scientific clarity.

Cannon, W. B. (1935). Stresses and strains of homeostasis (Mary Scott Newbold Lecture). *American Journal of Medical Sciences, 189,* 1-14.

Cannon's first use of the term *homeostasis*.

Selye, H. (1956). *The stress of life.* New York: McGraw-Hill.

Selye's most complete statement of his views on stress. A classic in the stress field.

Normal Physiological Regulation
The Autonomic Nervous System and Endocrine Outflow

In preparation for a discussion of stress, I will first review the mechanisms the body uses to maintain normal function.

Homeostatic regulation can be divided into four layers:

1. internal reflexes, by which organs regulate their own functions;
2. the autonomic nervous system and endocrine messengers, which act externally on the organs of the body;
3. the brainstem and hypothalamus, which integrate these autonomic and endocrine influences;
4. higher brain centers, brain areas above the hypothalamus that integrate emotional activity, memory, and awareness and that modulate the hypothalamus and brainstem.

In this chapter, I will consider the first three of these levels of control. In Chapter 5, I will discuss the concept of psychological stress and the similarities and differences with physical stressors. Chapter 6 addresses the influences imposed by the higher brain centers, their integration with emotions and

35

behavior, and their effects on stress mechanisms. Thus, I will spend three chapters developing an overview of how autonomic and endocrine responses operate normally, how they respond to physical threats to homeostasis, and how the system can be altered by psychological stimulation.

▓ Overview of Homeostatic Controls

In his discussion of the concept of homeostasis, Cannon (1935) proposes that the brainstem and hypothalamus receive information about the state of the bodily organs and maintain homeostasis by way of the autonomic nervous system and endocrine messengers. Figure 4.1 shows a view of the central nervous system, including the cerebral hemisphere and brainstem (inset), as well as the hypothalamus and pituitary gland. My description of the autonomic and endocrine systems is necessarily very brief. A highly readable, well-illustrated discussion of these systems is provided by Carlson (1991; especially Ch. 4).

A Hierarchy of Controls
on Vital Organs

At the most general level, the controls on the vital organs can be thought of as layered from the bottom up, forming successively higher levels of integration and organization. This system of controls is schematized in Figure 4.2. At the bottom are target tissues representing the various organs of the body innervated by the autonomic nervous system. The target tissues have intrinsic, reflex control mechanisms allowing them to operate without assistance when external conditions are constant. The organs alone cannot alter their function to meet rapid changes in demand or to coordinate their functions across organs, however. To do this, the system needs a way of sensing that conditions outside the separate organs have changed and a way of telling the vital organs to respond accordingly. Next are the ganglia of the autonomic nervous system. A ganglion is a collection of cell bodies and their interconnections within the peripheral nervous system. These may exert a limited degree of peripheral reflex control over the organs they serve. Above the autonomic ganglia is the reticular formation of the brainstem, a highly interconnected system of fibers and nuclei in the pons and medulla. These brainstem autonomic nuclei, in conjunction with endocrine secretions, provide the first level of integrated control over the target tissues. They are

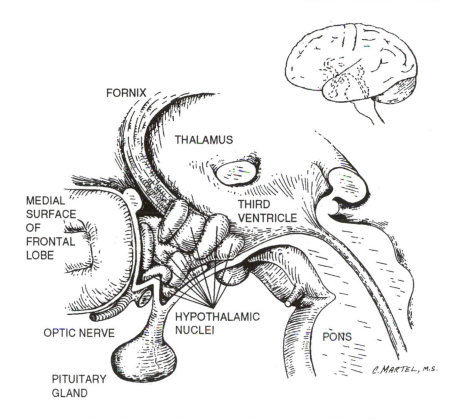

FORNIX

THALAMUS

MEDIAL
SURFACE
OF
FRONTAL
LOBE

THIRD
VENTRICLE

OPTIC NERVE

HYPOTHALAMIC
NUCLEI

PONS

C. MARTEL, M.S.

PITUITARY
GLAND

Figure 4.1. The central nervous system including the cerebral hemisphere, brainstem, and upper spinal cord. The hypothalamus, brainstem, and pituitary gland are outlined. An expanded view of the right side of the brain shows the hypothalamic nuclei, pituitary gland, medial surface of the frontal lobe, the pons, and the thalamus. The thalamus lies behind the plane of view here, next to the space formed by the third ventricle.

capable of adjusting to meet rapid changes in external conditions and to coordinate activity across organ systems.

The reticular formation, in turn, is modulated by the hypothalamus. Although the brainstem autonomic nuclei are fully capable of controlling autonomic reflexes, the hypothalamus is able to override these reflexes when necessary. Most important, the hypothalamus coordinates endocrine outflow and autonomic function. The hypothalamus receives blood-borne and nervous system inputs concerning the state of the body, such as oxygenation

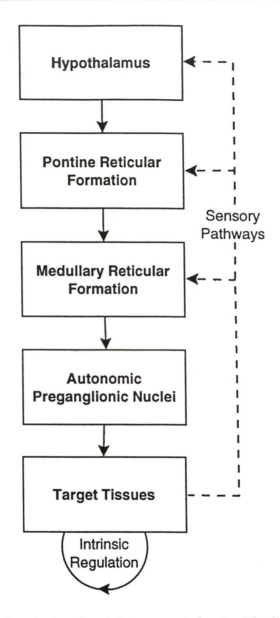

Figure 4.2. Organization of controls over organic function. The diagram indicates that individual organs have self-regulating capacity. This self-regulation is modulated by higher levels in the nervous system, including autonomic ganglia, medullary centers, pontine centers, and the hypothalamus.

and acidity of the blood, blood sugar, and body temperature. In response, it alters pituitary output to modulate metabolism, cardiovascular activity, and renal function, among others, and it alters the activity of brainstem autonomic reflex centers.

Finally, the hypothalamus receives descending inputs from the cortex and limbic system. These higher functions express the result of behavioral and emotional demands with powerful implications for hypothalamic, pituitary, and brainstem activity. These descending influences can lead to significant changes in bodily function, especially noticeable during states of psychological stress.

The hierarchical organization of autonomic controls has the virtue of allowing local processes that need little integration or external control to proceed on their own without the awareness of the person. An example is local regulation of blood flow by the action of local substances on the walls of blood vessels. This is an entirely local process that does not depend on external autonomic or endocrine regulation. At other times, it may be necessary for the local activity to be coordinated with the function of distant tissues to achieve a higher purpose. For example, the actions of the heart and blood vessels may need to be integrated for maximum performance during intense exercise. In this case, endocrine and integrated autonomic controls may come into play. At still other times, the awareness of the person may need to be brought to bear on the entire system to meet particular long-term needs. For example, a person who is jogging may recall that the exercise session has to end now because of family responsibilities, and so the lower autonomic centers and the exercising muscles receive the signal to slow down and head for home. The advantage of this arrangement is that things work fine by themselves and leave our limited conscious processing ability free for immediate tasks. This hierarchical arrangement illustrates, in a fairly ordinary way, how tissues and organs receive external messages only when needed. It also illustrates that the highest level of control is ultimately the cerebral cortex, which I will discuss in Chapter 6.

▨ Intrinsic Control Mechanisms

Each vital organ or organ system is capable of regulating its own function in response to slowly changing environmental demands. An example of the ability of an organ to regulate itself is the way the heart controls its own pumping action. First, the heart regulates its rate of contraction by its sinoatrial pacemaker node. This pacemaker node, located in the heart's atrial muscle, is a collection of specialized neurons that fire rhythmically at a very steady rate. By itself, the human heart will beat at about 110 beats per minute unless told to do otherwise by the autonomic nervous system or an endocrine messenger. Similarly, the force of the heart's contraction is locally regulated by an intrinsic property known as the *Frank-Starling mechanism*. The Frank-Starling response occurs as a result of the inherent property of the cardiac muscle to contract more effectively when stretched to a greater degree. As a result, the heart responds in proportion to the amount of blood returning to it from the systemic circulation. When more blood returns, the atrial chambers of the heart fill more completely before each beat, having greater stretch. This produces more effective filling of the ventricles and more stretch on their walls. The left ventricle therefore empties more completely, producing more effective flow into the aorta. In this manner, the heart keeps up with the flow demands placed on it by the systemic circulation. Finally, the heart's four chambers and system for regulating muscular contraction are physically designed to cause this complex organ to contract automatically in a coordinated manner. More detail on the cardiovascular system can be found in Guyton's (1992) textbook on human physiology.

The existence of these intrinsic cardiac controls means that if the heart is deprived of its autonomic innervation and its endocrine inputs, it will continue to supply blood to all the tissues of the body. It will maintain adequate blood flow completely on its own and without external control—as long as conditions remain constant. Unfortunately, if the individual possessing this functionally isolated heart were to do something so simple as to stand up suddenly, blood would move down into the legs and the amount of blood returning to the heart would drop precipitously. The heart would be uninformed that the state of the organism had changed and would be unable to increase its output of blood rapidly to respond to this brief, routine demand. Similarly, the blood vessels would not compensate for the sudden redistribution of the blood to the legs. As a result, the person might faint from a rapid drop in blood supply to the brain. So, although the heart's intrinsic controls are adequate to deal with constant conditions, such as when the person is sitting or lying down, rapid changes in demand must be met by additional controls supplied by endocrine and autonomic inputs.

This example of intrinsic cardiovascular control illustrates the sort of local controls possessed by other organ systems. It also shows that the autonomic and endocrine systems are in place to deal with threats to homeostasis resulting from rapid changes in external demands on the body.

■ Autonomic and Endocrine Controls

The autonomic and endocrine systems are functionally and anatomically distinct, but they act together to regulate and coordinate the activities of the bodily organs.

Three Autonomic Divisions

The autonomic nervous system innervates virtually every organ system in the body, as shown in Figure 4.3. It is a system of sensory and motor nerves, and it provides for the autonomous regulation of our vital organs without the need for voluntary intervention.

As a result of organized activity by the brainstem and hypothalamus, the autonomic nervous system sends control messages to the body by way of three anatomically and functionally distinct branches: the *sympathetic* nervous system, the *parasympathetic* nervous system, and the *enteric* nervous system. The autonomic nervous system is diagrammed in Figure 4.3. Here one can see both the brainstem and the spinal cord. The cord is divided into its cervical, thoracic, lumbar, and sacral segments, subdivided by the vertebrae.

Each division of the autonomic nervous system has four major components:

1. Preganglionic fibers. These are neuronal axons descending down the spinal cord, exiting at specific levels, and traveling to their respective ganglia.
2. Ganglia. As noted above, a ganglion is a collection of cell bodies and their interconnections within the peripheral nervous system. Ganglia constitute the primary way station for autonomic motor signals descending from the spinal cord and for sensory messages returning from the respective organs and tissues. They also are the first stage of integration of these forms of nerve activity.
3. Postganglionic fibers. These travel from the ganglia to the target tissues.

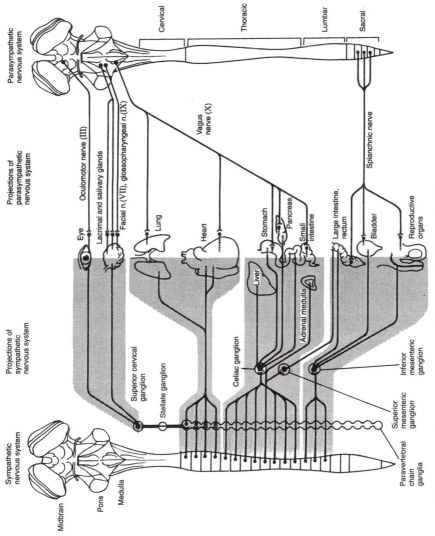

Figure 4.3. The autonomic nervous system and autonomically regulated organs.

Table 4.1	Autonomic Nervous System Effects on Target Organs	
Organ	*Sympathetic*	*Parasympathetic*
Eye	Pupillary dilation	Pupillary constriction
Saliva glands	Viscous saliva	Watery saliva
Lung	Bronchial dilation	Bronchial constriction
Heart	Increased rate, force	Decreased rate, force
Blood vessels	Constriction	No effect
Intestines	Decreased secretion and peristalsis	Increased secretion and peristalsis
Bladder	Relaxation	Contraction
Adrenal medulla	Epinephrine secretion	No effect

4. Neuroeffector junctions. These are the points at which descending signals act to alter the motor function of smooth muscles in the autonomically innervated organs. The neuroeffector junction has the character of a synapse between two neurons. At the junction, the nerve terminal secretes packets of its particular neurotransmitter and the neurotransmitter activates a smooth muscle or cardiac muscle cell by activating an appropriate receptor.

The branches of the autonomic nervous system act in concert, allowing a graded, reciprocal regulation of organic function. An example of this dual regulation is seen in the heart, where parasympathetic activity lessens the force and rate of contraction, whereas sympathetic activity increases these functions. Table 4.1 summarizes the effects of autonomic activity at major target organs.

The enteric nervous system acts primarily on the viscera of the digestive tract, and it consists primarily of local ganglia that receive inputs from a single organ and reflexively regulate the activity of that organ. Its neurotransmitter is acetylcholine.

The parasympathetic and sympathetic branches of the autonomic nervous system both send preganglionic neuronal fibers from the spinal cord to ganglia located outside the cord. At the ganglia, preganglionic fibers synapse with postganglionic fibers, which then travel to their respective target tissues. In all autonomic ganglia, the synaptic neurotransmitter is acetylcholine.

The Sympathetic
Nervous System

The sympathetic nervous system exits from the spinal cord at the thoracic and lumbar regions and sends preganglionic fibers to a series of interconnected ganglia known as the *paravertebral chain ganglia*. A preganglionic sympathetic fiber may synapse immediately with a postganglionic fiber, which in turn travels to its target organ, or the preganglionic fiber may travel up or down the chain ganglia before synapsing with postganglionic fibers. In fact, most sympathetic preganglionic fibers do both these things: They synapse with a postganglionic fiber at one level and send a collateral branch to another level in the chain, synapsing with several other postganglionic fibers along the way. In addition, some sympathetic preganglionics may travel directly to more distant ganglia controlling the actions of the digestive system, the large intestine, the bladder, and the genitalia.

In the sympathetic branch, each preganglionic fiber will synapse with an average of 10 postganglionic fibers. As a result of this 1:10 pre- to postganglionic ratio and the extensive linkages across ganglia, the activities of the sympathetic postganglionic fibers tend to be highly coordinated with each other. Accordingly, the actions of target organs tend to be closely integrated. In fact, the sympathetic branch was so named because of the concerted nature of its actions.

Sympathetic postganglionic fibers control the activity of smooth muscle or cardiac muscle by secreting norepinephrine at specialized neuroeffector junctions. The neuroeffector junction, similar to a synapse between nerves, is the interface between an autonomic nerve and its target tissue. It is here that a nerve impulse is translated into a motor action by the local tissue, allowing it to adjust its activity. At these junctions, norepinephrine acts primarily on α adrenoreceptors located on the surfaces of smooth muscle cells. The action of norepinephrine is to enhance the rate and force of contraction of the innervated smooth muscles. Thus, the sympathetic nervous system generally increases activation and function of the organs it supplies.

A notable exception to this description of pre- and postganglionic organization is the sympathetic innervation of the medulla of the adrenal glands, which are located above the kidneys. The adrenal medulla receives sympathetic preganglionic fibers directly from the spinal cord. These fibers secrete acetylcholine, as do all preganglionics, but they do not act on postganglionic fibers. Instead, this cholinergic stimulation causes the adrenal medulla to secrete the catecholamines epinephrine and norepinephrine into the bloodstream, where epinephrine acts as an endocrine messenger. Although norepinephrine is secreted into the circulation at the same time as epinephrine, its effect on tissues via the bloodstream is limited at best.

The sympathetic nervous system is always active. It plays an essential role in the body's adjustments to normal demands in concert with the parasympathetic nervous system, and it is essential for the integration and expression of the fight-flight response during times of stress. The *fight-flight response* is a highly integrated set of cardiovascular and endocrine changes designed to prepare for and support vigorous, even violent, physical activity involved in fighting or fleeing for one's life—just the sort of primitive behaviors designed to support survival in a threatening, life-or-death natural environment. This response is discussed later in more detail.

The Parasympathetic
Nervous System

The parasympathetic nervous system sends fibers to its target organs by way of the cranial nerves arising from the brainstem and by way of the sacral segment of the spinal cord. These fibers travel some distance from the cord to ganglia located close to, or inside, the target organs. This difference in the proximity of the ganglia to the target tissues is a major distinguishing feature of the parasympathetic system. Unlike the highly interconnected ganglia of the sympathetic branch, the parasympathetic ganglia are isolated from one another.

In addition to having widely separated ganglia, the parasympathetic nervous system has a small number of preganglionic fibers relative to postganglionic fibers. Each preganglionic fiber gives rise to an average of three postganglionics. This 1:3 ratio and separation of function among the ganglia suggests that activity at parasympathetic target tissues is highly localized and specific to the needs of the separate organs.

The postganglionic parasympathetic fibers act by secreting acetylcholine onto specialized cholinergic receptors located on smooth muscle fibers or, in the case of the heart, onto heart muscle and cardiac pacemakers to adjust the rate and force of the heart's contractions. In the gut, parasympathetic fibers stimulate gastric activity to permit digestion of food. In contrast to the sympathetic division's support of fight-or-flight responses, the para-sympathetic division generally supports feeding, energy storage, and repro-duction.

The Enteric Nervous System

The enteric branch of the autonomic nervous system is the most special-ized of the three. It is entirely embedded in the organs that it innervates: the gastrointestinal tract, the pancreas, and the gallbladder. These organs are able to act quite independently of outside control because their intrinsic sensory nerves communicate to sets of interneurons and motor output neurons able to control the organs in question. The entire enteric system is in turn controlled by the other two branches of the autonomic nervous system.

Endocrine Controls

The endocrine system consists of a collection of glands situated at various locations in the body, operating under the control of the pituitary gland and the autonomic nervous system. I will devote attention to two selected endocrine functions, the adrenocortical response and the adrenomedullary response because these have the greatest relevance to control over responses to stress and because they interact with immune system function. These endocrine responses are diagrammed in Figure 4.4.

The medulla of the adrenal gland is activated by sympathetic pregangli-onic fibers; in response, it secretes the catecholamine epinephrine into the systemic circulation. Epinephrine acts as an important endocrine messenger to many organ systems, where it acts on β adrenoreceptors located at points accessible to the diffusion of epinephrine from the bloodstream. In general, the action of epinephrine at β receptors reinforces the action of nor-epinephrine secreted by the sympathetic nerves supplied to the respective target organs. The fact that epinephrine travels via the general circulation allows it to act on many tissue sites at one time, thereby reinforcing the concerted actions of the sympathetic nerves. The secretion of epinephrine normally occurs at a very low rate, and its concentrations in the blood are consequently low. The rate of secretion of epinephrine increases selectively during states of stress, allowing it to coordinate several important functions subserving the behavioral and metabolic responses required to meet an

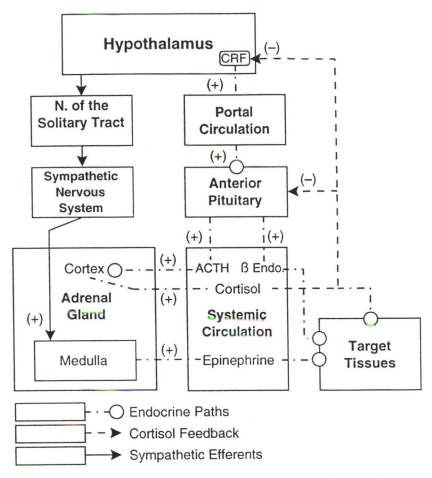

Figure 4.4. Neuroendocrine components of the stress response. Functional organization of the systems controlling release of the primary stress hormones cortisol and epinephrine.

emergency. For this reason, one may think of epinephrine as a key stress hormone.

Although norepinephrine is secreted along with epinephrine by the adrenal medulla, its actions on target tissues via the bloodstream are negligible. Its primary role is to act on target tissues by way of sympathetic nerve terminals.

The second major stress hormone is cortisol. In response to states of emergency, the hypothalamus secretes corticotropin releasing factor (CRF) into the specialized portal circulation of the pituitary stalk, where it travels to the anterior pituitary, causing the release of adrenocorticotropin (ACTH) and β endorphin into general circulation. ACTH travels to the adrenal cortex, where it causes a dramatic increase in the rate of production and secretion of the glucocorticoid hormone cortisol. Cortisol is capable of affecting every major organ system in the body and it is essential for the maintenance of normal organic and metabolic functions (Munck, Guyre, & Holbrook, 1984).

Cortisol's importance is indicated by the fact that it assists in many normal functions during both normal activity and stressful periods. During normal activity, the secretion of cortisol shows a very pronounced diurnal rhythm. Its secretion by the adrenal cortex reaches a peak before awakening, usually about 6:00 am, and levels drop slowly until about noon, where a small rise occurs prior to time for the midday meal. Cortisol levels vary over the afternoon hours and then decline to a low point at about 8:00-9:00 pm. This diurnal cycle is regulated by tonic activity from the hippocampus, acting through neuronal fibers reaching the paraventricular nucleus of the hypothalamus, causing it to stimulate CRF secretion. This tonic activity of the hippocampus is regulated by negative feedback of cortisol acting on specialized hippocampal receptors (not shown). Negative feedback is the most common form of regulation in the endocrine system. As its name implies, this form of feedback decreases the function of the target of the feedback. Negative feedback describes how a thermostat shuts off a furnace when the room temperature has risen to the level set at the control panel. An organism deprived of its adrenal cortex would not be able to live indefinitely without cortisol to assist in normal metabolic and cellular functions. For example, cortisol is necessary for the normal synthesis and function of both α and β adrenoreceptors. Without cortisol's presence, the actions of the autonomic nerves would be greatly diminished and circulating epinephrine would be less effective at its target tissues.

Cortisol also participates in the stress response. Stress levels of cortisol act to potentiate activities of the sympathetic nervous system, to increase the release of stored glucose and fats, and to suppress immune function. A partial list of cortisol's effects is provided in Table 4.2.

Table 4.2 Cortisol's Effects on Target Tissues

Tissues	Effect
Neuron	Enhanced catecholamine synthesis
Hippocampus	Enhanced memory function
Thalamus	Sensitivity to incoming stimuli
Adrenoreceptors	Enhanced α and β receptor sensitivity
Adrenal medulla	Enhanced catecholamine synthesis
Immune system	Enhanced and inhibited
Inflammation	Inhibited
Glucose	Enhanced production
Fatty acid	Enhanced liberation
Kidney	Water diuresis and sodium retention

Cortisol and epinephrine are able to integrate widespread functions due to their ability to reach all tissues via the systemic circulation and thereby to alter significantly the background environment in which those tissues operate. In addition to the integration of organic function achieved by the opposing dual effects of sympathetic and parasympathetic fibers, simultaneous endocrine influences modulate and coordinate activity and responses across many tissues.

β endorphin, which is released by the pituitary in equal quantities along with ACTH, is a potent agonist of opiate receptors in the nervous system, producing analgesia, among other effects. Because β endorphin is released along with cortisol during stress, it appears to act as an analgesic in preparation for potential pain or injury and possibly to regulate moods during such times.

Integration and Higher Control of Autonomic Function

The output of the major branches of the autonomic nervous system is regulated in the brainstem by the nucleus of the solitary tract, acting in conjunction with a variety of other autonomic nuclei. The outputs to the periphery are transmitted to the autonomic ganglia via the cranial nerves and the intermediolateral cell column of the spinal cord. The brainstem control nuclei are found in the reticular formation of the medulla and pons.

The Brainstem Reticular Formation

The reticular formation is a network of neurons found throughout the core of the brainstem. It may be divided into two functional subsystems: the aminergic nuclei and the autonomic control nuclei.

Aminergic Nuclei of the Reticular Formation

The aminergic nuclei are separate clusters of neuronal cell bodies synthesizing the neurotransmitters serotonin, norepinephrine, and dopamine. These nuclei regulate sleeping, waking, attention, mood, and modulation of sensory input. The serotonergic and dopaminergic nuclei are thought to play critical roles in regulating moods and attention. These global functions of the aminergic nuclei account for the traditional view that the reticular formation subserves generalized activation of behavior and nervous system function. The aminergic nuclei have the ability to alter activity in widespread areas of the central nervous system. They are also responsible in gross changes in alertness, ranging from drowsiness to normal waking to extreme alertness. For this reason, it has been tempting in the fields of psychology and physiology to invoke the concept of activation or arousal to explain such major changes in behavioral state. The contemporary view acknowledges that there is no simple, unidimensional activation process ranging from low to high, however. Instead, it has been more useful to consider how specific brain systems become active to meet specific demands.

The neurotransmitters of the respective aminergic nuclei are (1) norepinephrine, synthesized by the locus ceruleus; (2) serotonin, synthesized by the raphe nuclei; and (3) dopamine, synthesized by the cell bodies of the ventral tegmental area. The axons of each of these collections of cell bodies project to all parts of the cerebral cortex, the limbic system, and the cerebellum and spinal cord. As an exception, dopaminergic neurons originating in the ventral tegmental area project only to the cortex. These nuclei are therefore able to modulate the state of the central nervous system by the patterns of secretion of their transmitters at widespread sites in the brain and spinal cord.

A key nucleus in the central nervous system's elaboration of the response to stress is the locus ceruleus. The locus ceruleus contains 90% of the norepinephrine-containing fibers in the central nervous system, and these project to every part of the cerebral cortex; to limbic structures, such as the hippocampus and amygdala; and to the spinal cord. This distribution suggests that the locus ceruleus has a generalized role in modulating and coordinating the functional state and activity of many parts of the central nervous system. As I will discuss in Chapter 6, the locus ceruleus has important reciprocal relations with the amygdala of the limbic system and with the hypothalamic centers integrating stress responses.

The serotonergic raphe nuclei are also of great significance for the establishment of mood. A deficient supply of serotonin or a lack of serotonin receptors results in a preponderance of negative moods and feelings of anger and aggressive behaviors.

Autonomic Control Nuclei
of the Reticular Formation

The reticular formation also contains a series of specialized autonomic control nuclei. These receive inputs from various bodily organs and higher centers in the nervous system. A partial list includes the nucleus paragigantocellularis, which serves posture and locomotion; the nucleus of the solitary tract, which is responsible for baroreceptor regulation of blood pressure; and the intermediolateral cell column, a complex of cell bodies extending from the pons through the medulla to the spinal cord that carries afferent sympathetic information to the sympathetic ganglionic chain.

An example of autonomic reflex control is seen in the control of blood pressure. When blood pressure rises, the baroreceptors in the aorta and carotid arteries detect increased stretch on the walls of the vessels. They signal the nucleus of the solitary tract to send signals to the vagal motor nucleus of the medulla, telling it to raise the firing rate of the vagus nerve innervating the parasympathetic ganglion controlling heart rate. The ganglion causes the parasympathetic postganglionic fibers to increase their firing rate, thus inhibiting the rate of the sinoatrial node of the heart. As a result, heart rate goes down and blood pressure drops.

As a broad generalization, these brainstem nuclei provide adequate reflex control over single organs and certain systems, such as the cardiovascular system. Their reflex control is not well coordinated across organs or between systems, however. To accomplish this integrative control, it is desirable to coordinate these nuclei and control endocrine secretions. This autonomic-endocrine coordination is accomplished by the hypothalamus.

The Hypothalamus

The hypothalamus is frequently described as the head ganglion of the autonomic nervous system; the cluster of nuclei forming this area is diagrammed in Figure 4.1 (FitzGerald, 1992).

The hypothalamus has two functional divisions: the endocrine and the autonomic. The autonomic division activates or inhibits the autonomic control centers of the brainstem. Studies have shown that electrical stimulation of the anterior areas of the hypothalamus enhances parasympathetic outflow to the cardiovascular system, leading to decreased heart rate and lowered blood pressure. In contrast, stimulation of posterior hypothalamic centers produces sympathetically mediated increases in heart rate and blood pressure. Axons from the hypothalamus reach the nucleus of the solitary tract of the brainstem and the intermediolateral cell column of the spinal cord. This example illustrates that the functionally complete cardiovascular reflexes controlled by the brainstem can be modified by higher control exerted by the hypothalamus. This arrangement allows the cardiovascular system to be regulated by the reflex mechanisms of the pons and medulla, and also to respond to other demands communicated to and through the hypothalamus.

The second major hypothalamic division provides control of the pituitary gland. The pituitary is divided anatomically into its anterior and posterior parts. The anterior pituitary is controlled by hypothalamic endocrine secretions arriving by way of the portal circulation. The posterior pituitary receives direct input from these hypothalamic secretory nerve fibers. These fibers secrete directly into capillary vessels that connect to the systemic circulation.

Two important stress-related endocrine messengers secreted by the hypothalamus are CRF and arginine vasopressin (AVP). As noted above, CRF travels to the anterior pituitary to allow for the secretion of ACTH. AVP (also known as antidiuretic hormone) is released at the posterior pituitary, where it enters the general circulation to control the rate of excretion of water by the kidneys. Anatomically distinct populations of neurons of the paraventricular nucleus of the hypothalamus synthesize CRF only, AVP only, or both CRF and AVP. The CRF-AVP neurons play a major role in the stress response by greatly enhancing the pituitary's output of ACTH (Petrusz & Merchenthaler, 1992). Their actions are discussed in greater detail in Chapter 6.

SUMMARY

Considering control over organic function, starting with the intrinsic controls by the organs and moving up through the ganglia, spinal cord, brainstem, and hypothalamus, one gains an appreciation that the vital functions of the body are functionally autonomous, with regulation and integrated controls being applied in a layered fashion as one moves up the system. This hierarchical control scheme is designed to coordinate the activities of otherwise isolated tissues and organs and organize their function in increasingly concerted ways so that their integrated actions may serve higher purposes. Although these controls need no voluntary intervention to operate properly, they are subject to intervention by higher control centers. These intervening controls are emphasized in Chapter 6, when I consider higher mental and emotional functions that act on this organizational scheme from the top down.

In terms of my larger agenda to describe the role of psychological stress as a modifier of the actions of the body—or, as I said before, to answer the question of how an idea can change the body—I will later describe the modification of these autonomic and endocrine activities by the higher brain centers made up by the cortex and limbic system.

FURTHER READING

Cannon, W. B. (1935). Stresses and strains of homeostasis (Mary Scott Newbold Lecture). *American Journal of Medical Sciences, 189,* 1-14.

This is a basic statement of Cannon's views on homeostasis.

Carlson, N. R. (1991). *Physiology of behavior* (4th ed.). Boston: Allyn & Bacon.

This is a basic text providing broad discussion of physiology in relation to behavior. It has highly readable sections on the hypothalamus, brainstem, and autonomic nervous system, as well as on emotional stress.

Dodd, J., & Role, L. W. (1991). The autonomic nervous system. In E. R. Kandel, J. H. Schwartz, & T. M. Jessell (Eds.), *Principles of neural science* (3rd ed., pp. 761-775). New York: Elsevier Science.

This is a comprehensive yet brief description of the autonomic nervous system.

FitzGerald, M. J. T. (1992). *Neuroanatomy: Basic and clinical.* London: Ballière Tindall.

This is a well-illustrated and readable text on truly functional aspects of neuroanatomy.

Physiological Regulation During Physical and Psychological Stress

To consider the possible effects of long-term stress on the body, I will first examine the acute changes that occur during brief periods of stress. This information helps answer the original question about how ideas can have power over bodies and how stress mechanisms can affect disease processes. In this chapter, I will take a detailed look at two major types of stressors. The first type includes physical exercise and fight-flight situations. The second type includes mental stressors, illustrated by work on challenging psychomotor tasks and the mental arithmetic task.

Because of my interest in psychological aspects of stress, I examine these representative stressors in terms of the top-down versus bottom-up nature of their activational properties. On the one extreme is physical exercise, which produces pronounced cardiovascular and endocrine responses primarily because of bottom-up, physical demands of the working muscles sending ascending signals to the brain. On the other extreme is mental arithmetic, which involves top-down activation due to intense mental effort to perform arithmetic calculations in working memory. This ability to activate cardiovascular control centers in the brainstem is related to signals from higher centers. The top-down organization of such stressors provides the beginnings of a working model of psychological stress.

I will also consider each stressor in terms of its activating and appetitive-aversive qualities. The total physiological response to a behavioral challenge results from activation associated with the demands of the situation and the emotions it evokes.

▓ Classes of Stress Responses

There are several schemes for classifying stressors. Here I have chosen to consider physical versus psychological stressors and to view their effects in terms of activation and appetitive-aversive qualities. I should note that studies of stress in animals have yielded two major patterns of reaction to stressor challenge. The first pattern concerns cases of threat to control, in which the organism is actively striving to maintain or gain control over the environment. Threat to control evokes either an immediate assertion of control over the situation or an effortful attempt to gain control. The physiological response during such active efforts to control the environment is known as the *defense reaction*. The examples of exercise and fight-flight response discussed in this chapter fall into this category. As I have noted, however, the emotions involved may differ between the two. The second pattern concerns situations of actual loss of control over the environment. These have been termed the *defeat reaction*. In Chapter 7, I consider the effects of loss of control and the resulting experience of helplessness and its effects on persons and animals. A short review of this classification scheme and some major components of the physiological responses during each situation is provided by Folkow (1993).

The animal literature contains a significant number of studies comparing defense reactions with defeat reactions. Many of these studies involve aggressive encounters between two members of a species and an examination of the physiological responses on the part of the winner and the loser of these encounters. The exact responses in each case are complex because, for each species, a unique set of social relations determines all aspects of the behavioral interaction between individuals. For example, chimpanzees, who live in social groups, have very different rules for determining dominance and the nature of aggressive encounters than do orangutans, which are more solitary and less likely to have aggressive encounters. Similarly, leaf-eating monkeys have different levels of activity and aggression than fruit-eating monkeys. Factors such as social conditions and food type interact with a historically determined set of relationships between individuals and their conspecific aggressors and natural predators. These well-developed interactions have related endocrine and physiological adjustments that differ somewhat across species. Weiner (1992, Ch. 7) discusses this point. In this chapter, I focus on exercise and fight-flight situations as two variations on the defense reaction.

▓ The Exercise Response

Exercise has two major components: (1) the *preparatory phase* and (2) the *active phase*. During exercise, substantial changes occur in cardiovascular activity and hormonal output. The purpose of these adjustments is to provide maximum oxygen and fuel to the exercising muscles. An excellent review of the exercise response can be found in Smith, Guyton, Manning, and White (1976). A brief overview of cardiovascular function may be found in Rushmer (1989), and more detail may be found in Guyton (1992).

The Preparatory Phase of Exercise

Physiologists have noted that humans and nonhumans preparing for exercise often show dramatic changes in physiological function before significant muscular activity is undertaken. This has led to the recognition that centrally generated commands from the cortex can result in altered hypothalamic and brainstem functions controlling autonomic outflow (Hobbs, 1982). These preparatory changes mimic changes that occur during exercise. For example, in trained runners preparing to start an actual race, resting heart rates were found to more than double as the starter was calling out the starting commands (McArdle, Foglia, & Patti, 1967). The rise in heart rate was greatest in sprinters starting a 60-yard dash (67 to 148 beats per minute), smaller in preparation for a 220-yard dash (67 to 130 beats per minute), and still less in middle-distance runners before starting an 880-yard run (62 to 122 beats per minute).

Evidence from animal studies shows that the preparatory phase is initiated in the prefrontal cortex, suggesting activation of a planned, intentional set of preparatory changes. Activity in the prefrontal cortex then gives rise to increased activity of the supplementary motor cortex, the premotor cortex, and the primary motor cortex (FitzGerald, 1992).

These cortical changes result in descending influences that activate the hypothalamus and brainstem nuclei associated with sympathetic activation and suppression of parasympathetic activity. These changes result in increased heart rate, increased cardiac output, increased sympathetic outflow to the blood vessels, and increased epinephrine secretion. There is some uncertainty about the amount of vasoconstriction of the blood vessels accompanying preparation for exercise. It is likely that some combination of circulating epinephrine and autonomically mediated changes causes dilation of some muscle vascular beds, resulting in increased muscle blood flow. The net effect of these changes is an increase in blood pressure, with a proportionally greater rise in systolic pressure relative to diastolic pressure. The top-down nature of these cortical influences is illustrated by the active inhibition of the baroreceptor reflex by cortical influences, as described in Chapter 4.

I will return to a discussion of the preparatory phase after describing the changes actually occurring during exercise. These anticipatory changes will provide a basis for thinking about mental stress and its effects on the body.

The Active Phase of Exercise

During the initiation of exercise, muscular work commences, with the result that the descending cerebral influences in the preparatory phase are now enhanced by (1) neural feedback from muscular contraction, (2) peripherally induced changes in blood vessel function, and (3) return of blood to the heart. The combination of muscle contraction, vascular dilation, and increased sympathetic function results in significant increases in cardiac output, amounting to as much as six times resting levels. As a result, cardiac output may rise from about 4 L/min in a resting adult man to 24 L/min at maximum exercise (see Smith et al., 1976, for a complete discussion). These changes in cardiac output during exercise result from a combination of centrally induced motor commands acting on autonomic centers and feedback from the periphery, but the larger influence is the peripheral one.

Peripheral Blood Flow in Exercise

Sympathetic outflow to all the blood vessels increases substantially during exercise. As a result, blood flow in nonworking muscles does not change appreciably from resting values, and blood flow to the viscera actually decreases. This generalized increase in vascular tonus also results in increased tension on the walls of the large veins that conduct blood back to the heart, thereby improving the return of blood to the heart. In spite of increased sympathetically mediated constriction of the blood vessels in nonworking muscles and the viscera, however, local mechanisms ensure that an adequate supply of blood reaches the working muscles. The exercising muscles produce metabolites due to their increased use of oxygen and fuel. These metabolites result in relaxation of the muscle layer of the resistance vessels of the working muscles, causing substantial increases in blood flow, which may reach eight times resting levels.

This combination of descending autonomic influences and local metabolic influences results in a redistribution of blood flow, allowing significant increases of oxygen and nutrients to reach the exercising muscles. As a result of these increases, a trained runner may maintain 85% of maximum effort for periods of 3 to 5 hours.

Cardiac Output During Exercise

The other major component of the cardiovascular adjustment to exercise involves profound changes in the activity of the heart.

First, the improved return of blood to the heart results in better filling of the left ventricle during the brief period of relaxation prior to each beat. This improved filling results in greater stretch of the muscular wall of the atria and ventricles. It is a basic property of cardiac muscle that it contracts more effectively in response to increased stretch, a response known as the *Frank-Starling reflex.* Therefore, the redistribution of blood volume and flow caused by sympathetic output and increased muscle metabolism results in improvement of the pumping action of the heart. This results in an increased stroke volume, which is the amount of blood the heart expels on each beat.

Second, during exercise, the increase in feedback from exercising muscle to the brainstem cardiovascular control centers results in a suppression of parasympathetic activity and an increase in sympathetic outflow from the brainstem cardiovascular control centers, as noted above. This shift to a dominant sympathetic pattern of outflow results in a substantial increase in heart rate. Highly trained athletes may have resting heart rates of 35 to 40 beats per minute, whereas during exercise they may maintain sustained rates of 180 beats per minute, indicating a four- to fivefold increase.

Third, the contractile force of the heart may increase during exercise. This results from (1) increased sympathetic outflow to the heart acting to improve contractile force of the left ventricle, and (2) the increase in circulating epinephrine, which augments this improved contractility by acting on β adrenergic receptors on cardiac muscle (described in the next section).

One therefore sees three influences acting in concert to improve the action of the heart as a pump: improved filling of the left ventricle, increased frequency of contraction, and increased force of contraction. These lead to increased cardiac output and increased blood flow to the working muscles.

Endocrine Changes During Exercise

Sympathetic changes in cardiovascular activity during exercise are accompanied by supporting changes in endocrine function. Endocrine responses enhance cardiovascular function directly and support muscular work by increasing the availability of fuel.

Epinephrine, secreted by the adrenal medulla, acts to augment autonomically mediated changes in the heart and blood vessels. First, epinephrine increases cardiac contractility, as already noted. Second, it increases dilation of blood vessels in exercising muscles by acting on β adrenoreceptors in the blood vessel wall. This works to decrease vascular resistance in exercising muscles, augmenting the metabolic dilation mentioned above. Third, epinephrine increases the liberation of stored fat, allowing free fatty acids to enter the circulation and travel to exercising muscles for utilization as fuel.

Cortisol, secreted by the cortex of the adrenal gland located above the kidney, is critical for the liberation of stored glucose and fat. Sometime after the onset of exercise, the increased use of circulating glucose as fuel for the muscles will result in a drop in blood glucose levels. This is a signal to the hypothalamus and pituitary to increase the release of adrenocorticotropin (ACTH) to signal increased production of cortisol. Cortisol then acts to increase the liberation into the bloodstream of glucose from the liver and free fatty acids from adipose tissues.

β endorphin is secreted by the pituitary in equal amounts along with ACTH. β endorphin is known to be an opiate analogue and to activate brain receptor sites associated with opioid analgesia. It may also have mood elevating effects. This system is thought to modulate the discomfort associated with severe muscle effort and to modulate moods during fight-flight situations.

Exercise and Adaptation to Stress

Selye (1936) recognizes that exposure to a stressor can increase the body's ability to cope with that stressor in the future by a process of physiological adaptation. Exercise is an excellent example of increased coping with repeated exposure. Physical training involves doing a set of exercises with increasing intensity over an extended period. The increase in ability with training is an example of adaptation to the required effort.

Selye (1936) also notes that severe and extended exposure to any stressor can ultimately exceed the ability of the system to cope or adapt. Similarly, it is possible for a person who enjoys exercise to increase the level of physical demand from session to session beyond the body's ability to respond adaptively and recover fully, making the exercise a source of long-term physical stress. Runners habitually training more than 45 miles per week at moderate to high intensity are known to have chronically elevated cortisol levels and negative mood states (Luger et al., 1987). Too much physical training can produce a state of overtraining that may take months of abstinence from exercise for full recovery.

The Fight-Flight Response

As Bernard (1961) postulates, all living systems must have methods of self-protection, whether that means compensating for minor variations in the temperature, fighting off invading organisms, or fleeing from a predator. As organisms became more complex, so did the repertoire of responses that could be used to fend off harm. It seems reasonable that organisms better equipped to defend themselves would have a survival and evolutionary advantage over those less equipped. Physiologists and psychologists use the term *fight-flight response* in reference to this loosely defined constellation of functions.

I consider the fight-flight response a prototype stress response. It is an energetically intense set of behavioral and physiological changes, undertaken in the interest of maintaining life in the most acutely threatening circumstances. The fight-flight response incorporates powerful emotional components and equally powerful exercise-related neuroendocrine and physiological changes.

The emotions associated with fight or flight are normally considered unpleasant or negative. These include (1) anxiety, a sense of apprehension, and the anticipation of physical harm; (2) fear, a stronger form of anxiety, often felt in the presence of the threat itself; and (3) anger, an outward-directed destructive impulse. These emotions, accompanied by neuroendocrine and physiological reactions, motivate adaptive behaviors during threatening circumstances. A primary component of all fight-flight situations is that the organism has limited control over the outcome: It is not certain at the outset that serious injury or death can be avoided. In fact, capture and the helplessness associated with forced immobility are known to be among the most profound of aversive stressors. Tonic immobilization of an experimental animal is therefore used as a highly reproducible and useful laboratory stressor.

The endocrine changes associated with the emotions during fight or flight are generally those that increase the vigor and strength of overt behavior, intensify the physiological reactions, and assist in the liberation of energy stores to enhance the likelihood of successful flight or fight. Recall that endocrine substances are transported by the blood to all tissues in the body, and they have the ability to integrate widespread elements of complex responses. The primary hormones underlying the fight-flight response are cortisol, β endorphin, and epinephrine.

The autonomic nervous system changes associated with the fight-flight response are a general suppression of parasympathetic activity and increased sympathetic activity. This implies a shift from the energy storing and conserving functions served by the parasympathetic branch to an emphasis on the energy expending functions associated with gross muscular activity and physical effort necessary to flee from or struggle with an opponent. These changes are the same as would occur during exercise, and the information on autonomic changes during exercise may be applied equally well here.

The fight-flight response may also be divided into preparatory and active phases similar to the two phases of the exercise response. For example, Anderson and Tosheff (1973) modeled the preparatory and active phases of an aversive encounter by exposing dogs to an active avoidance procedure (active phase) versus having the dogs wait for a prolonged period in the apparatus prior to the avoidance (preparation). The avoidance period was characterized by elevated blood pressure along with increased cardiac output and decreased peripheral resistance, an exercise-like pattern. During preparation, the blood pressure was elevated primarily by increased vascular resistance, with a small decrease in cardiac output. These phases clearly parallel the preparation for exercise and the active phases of exercise described above, although the preavoidance period appears to be characterized by higher levels of peripheral resistance than exercise preparation.

For my purposes, the active portion of the fight-flight response involves vigorous exercise accompanied by negative emotions and significant elevation of cortisol, β endorphin, and epinephrine.

▒ Different Emotions and Motivations Accompanying the Exercise and Fight-Flight Responses

The review of the exercise response, both the preparatory and active phases, indicates that the body is capable of substantial adjustments to the demands of vigorous activity. One may think of the exercise response as forming the core of the fight-flight response. There is a crucial difference between exercise, however, particularly for enjoyment, and fight-flight situations in the motivational state and the emotions accompanying each activity.

Most people choose to exercise for positive reasons. They run, swim, or engage in competition for enjoyment and improved health. The exercising person may feel significant positive emotions, along with freedom and an intense sense of satisfaction. Such exercise is voluntary, and the person has almost complete control over its duration and intensity. The outcomes, short of accidental injury, carry significant benefits and few costs. Prolonged strenuous exercise may also produce a metabolically induced secretion of ACTH accompanied by β endorphin secretion. The mood alterations associated with β endorphin are often referred to as a *runner's high*. Therefore, exercise may produce largely positive moods, and the associated endocrine changes are primarily a result of demands for fuel by the muscles.

In the case of the fight-flight response, an organism is fleeing or fighting for its existence. The attendant emotions, such as anxiety, fear, and anger, are powerful negative ones. The behavioral outcome of such an encounter is uncertain, and the costs of failure are disastrous. Such situations produce an immediate and substantial elevation of ACTH, β endorphin, and cortisol. In contrast, during exercise, the changes in these hormones are induced by the elevated energy demands and are confined to feedback mechanisms at the hypothalamus and pituitary. The changes occurring during fight-flight involve descending activation via the frontal cortex and emotion centers in the limbic system, especially the amygdala and septohippocampal complex. In Chapter 7, I review studies of humans and animals showing the effects of uncertainty in the face of aversive events. I also discuss research showing profound behavioral, physiological, and neurochemical alterations in animals following prolonged exposure to uncontrollable aversive stimuli such as electric shock. These studies tell us that significant emotionally relevant secretion of stress hormones may occur due to loss of control over the environment, the high cost of failure, and negative emotions.

These issues of control, negative emotions, and endocrine secretion help answer a question frequently asked about stress and exercise. Because stress is usually portrayed as undesirable, it is natural to question why exercise is so often prescribed as beneficial for health and mood enhancement. The answer lies in the motivations and emotions involved in the situation. Exercise is a physical challenge, undertaken in graded doses and allowing the person complete control over the outcome. As long as the person avoids overtraining, exercise may increase physical fitness and often improves mood. This degree of control and the differences in the accompanying emotions make exercise different from true fight-flight situations.

The effect of a stressor depends heavily on the way the person interprets the situation at hand. Two challenges that are equally physically demanding can have different consequences for the individual based on the interpretation of the situation and the accompanying emotions. Mason (1968, 1975a, 1975b) performed an extensive series of laboratory studies of adaptive mechanisms and stress responses in primates. One of his most pervasive findings is that monkeys produce high levels of cortisol when exposed to novel challenges in the laboratory, but that this response disappears when the situation becomes familiar. Mason concludes that the novelty of each situation is a major determinant of its stressor value, suggesting that the psychological reaction to the situation is as important, or more important, than the event itself.

Psychological Stress

If one considers the sources of threat to the integrity of the organism, the most obvious sources are the kinds of physical stressors that Selye (1936) was mainly concerned with: cold, heat, infection, hemorrhage, and the like. I refer to these as *physical stressors* because they are threats based on their physical ability to cause harm or destroy life. Psychologists and other students of behavior are more often interested in *psychological stressors*. By these I mean challenges that can alter the workings of the body, and perhaps affect health, because of their meaning to the person and the effect of these meanings in the person's daily life. Psychological stressors include such events as loss of a loved one, failure to achieve a highly valued goal in life, or a turn for the worse in a significant relationship. These can be acute, traumatic events or long-lasting strains. Such challenges clearly do not pose a threat because they are physically harmful in the way that cold is, and so one should consider what mechanism allows a piece of bad news to bring on a crushing sense of oppression, perhaps tears and sorrow, a loss of faith in the future, and even illness.

As a start, I turn to the example above of the anticipation of exercise. The cardiovascular responses occurring in anticipation of exercise are interesting because they provide a glimpse of the possibility that widespread changes can occur in peripheral function exclusively because of changes in brain activity associated with thinking about and preparing for movement. Smith and his colleagues (Smith et al., 1993) provide impressive data from primates (rhesus macaques) living in social groups and instrumented to provide real-time readouts of physiological activity along with detailed videotaped records of their behavior. These records show substantial rises in heart rate and blood pressure in monkeys sitting still—immediately preceding attacking another monkey. Similarly to the preparation for exercise, these cardiovascular changes illustrate the power of the descending influences of an evolving plan of attack, including presumed emotions such as anger or hostility, to significantly alter the state of the body.

Mental Arithmetic as a
Prototypical Mental Stressor

The mental arithmetic task, used by Brod (1963) in a series of influential studies in hypertensives, is really a family of tasks requiring the volunteer to calculate answers to arithmetic problems without benefit of paper and pencil and to provide accurate answers as a check on performance. One example is to give the subject a three-digit number and ask him or her to add the digits together and then add the sum to the original number. The answer is yet another three-digit number, and the same calculations are repeated on each new number until the end of the task period. All versions of the task require the subject to devote significant processing resources to working memory. This is an effortful process that can be mildly unpleasant after the first few seconds. The characteristics of the task can be readily manipulated to increase the difficulty of the calculations and the error rates and to alter positive or negative emotional valence.

Mental arithmetic produces significant decreases in vagal tone to the heart and increases in sympathetically mediated cardiac activity (Hedman, Hjemdahl, Nordlander, & Åström, 1990). This results in significant increases in heart rate and contractility. Vascular resistance is unchanged or slightly increased from baseline (Allen, Obrist, Sherwood, & Crowell, 1987). These cardiovascular changes are primarily due to the mental effort involved, although blood pressure responses are enhanced by the effect of speaking the answers aloud (Linden, 1991). The task is perceived as mildly aversive (al'Absi, Lovallo, McKey, & Pincomb, 1994), and it produces significant increases in cortisol secretion into the bloodstream (al'Absi et al., 1994; Williams et al., 1982). One can therefore think of the mental arithmetic task as a prototype psychological stressor. It produces significant cardiovascular activation, along with mild aversion and cortisol secretion. It does these things in the face of minimal motor demands and maximal mental effort. Its ability to alter physiological function, to have an effect on the workings on the body, derives almost exclusively from the activation of brain centers capable of affecting the brainstem and hypothalamic-pituitary axis. These areas are discussed in detail in Chapter 6.

▓ Responses to Aversive and Nonaversive Challenges

I have noted that mental arithmetic is perceived as mildly aversive and that it results in increased cortisol secretion. As a way of illustrating the importance of the emotional response to a challenge, I present in detail the results of two companion studies that called on human volunteers to perform tasks with nearly identical physical requirements but having substantial differences in their psychological components (Lovallo, Pincomb, & Wilson, 1986b; Lovallo et al., 1985).

In the first study (Lovallo et al., 1985), we were interested in knowing how human volunteers would react to aversive stimuli when trying to control their occurrence under conditions of maximum uncertainty. One could think of the aversive character and lack of control in this experiment as evoking the psychological components of the fight-flight response. In the second study, the subjects performed a nearly identical task, but this time they could earn money for good performance and there were no aversive penalties (Lovallo et al., 1986b). One may look at this task in terms of an activational state of working for a positive outcome, with little chance of a negative outcome. The psychological difference between these two tasks parallels the psychological difference between exercise as a positive challenge and fight-flight as a fear-ridden and uncertain struggle.

Exposure to Noise and Shock

In the first study (Lovallo et al., 1985), young adult men were asked to perform a simple psychomotor task to avoid the presentation of two aversive stimuli, noise and electric shock. The shocks were brief, mild ones known to be safe and harmless. Nevertheless, even mild electric shock feels unpleasant. The noise was brief enough to permit safe levels of exposure but intense enough to produce a strong degree of startle. The psychomotor task was a 15-minute, simple, variable-interval reaction time task in which the subjects pressed a response key whenever a red light in front of them came on. There were 24 trials, ranging from 4 to 90 seconds between respond signals, and these signals occurred without warning. In addition, the subject was uncertain when a response would be called for and when a response would be fast enough to avoid an unpleasant outcome. Although the subjects were told that if they responded rapidly enough they would avoid receiving an electric shock or noise burst, in fact these were preprogrammed to occur unpredictably on 50% of the trials (4 shocks and 8 noise bursts). The subjects were also told that if they responded slowly, they might or might not receive a shock or noise burst. This prevented the subjects from testing the relationship between reaction time and aversive stimulation. So from the subject's point of view, this task involved anxiety, fear, and maximum uncertainty about the timing and exact source of an aversive event. At the same time, in an attempt to avoid unpleasant outcomes, the subject had to maintain continuous attention for the full 15 minutes, to be prepared to react as rapidly as possible at any moment, and to make rapid motor responses.

This attempt to cope with the aversive challenge produced changes very much like the model of a fight-flight response. The subjects experienced the task as being activating (reporting increased concentration, effort, interest, and tenseness), as would be expected where effort was being expended to control events, and distressing (less control and pleasantness and more distress, impatience, and irritation), as would be normal for exposure to aversive stimuli. The cardiovascular pattern, presented in Figure 5.1a, shows increased systolic and diastolic blood pressure. The hemodynamic adjustments underlying this blood pressure rise show a drop in vascular resistance and an increase in all components of cardiac performance, including increased heart rate and cardiac output and increased contractile indices, including a rise in Heather's index of contractility and a shortened preejection period. This pattern of subjective and cardiovascular changes was accompanied by significant alterations in neuroendocrine function. Norepinephrine levels in the blood increased significantly, indicating enhanced global sympathetic function. Cortisol levels also increased significantly. We found that baseline cortisol was significantly correlated with reports of distress, and poststress cortisol was related to distress, tension, and irritability.

It should be emphasized that the subjects were sitting still in a recliner chair with their legs elevated for the entire study. The rises in norepinephrine and cortisol suggest a centrally mediated set of responses related to negative emotions and preparation for a fight-flight response, not due to elevated energy expenditure.

Work to Earn Monetary Reward

In our second study (Lovallo et al., 1986b), we challenged the subjects with a rewarding, nonaversive version of the same reaction time task. The

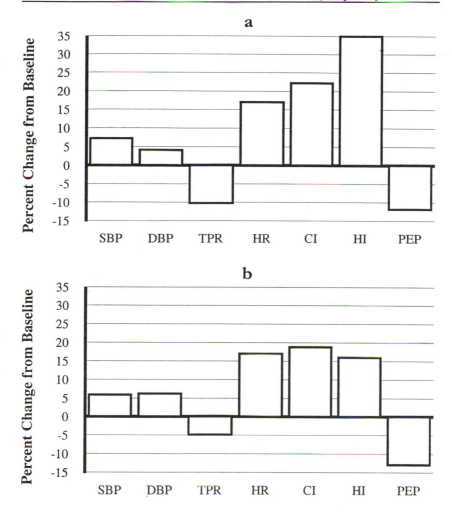

Figure 5.1. Cardiovascular responses during reaction time tasks requiring sustained attention and preparation to carry out rapid motor responses.
(a) Reaction time task using electric shock and loud noise as incentives.
(b) Reaction time task using monetary bonuses as incentives.

major difference was that instead of threat of noise or shock as a motivator, we paid subjects $.50 bonuses for each very rapid response (less than 270 msec) they could perform. The behavioral requirements were the same as for the aversive task. Subjects had to maintain extreme alertness to detect the onset of a respond light, they had to be at a heightened state of preparedness, and they had to make rapid button presses to earn rewards.

The results, shown in Figure 5.1b, show the same pattern of cardiovascular change that the aversive task does: Blood pressure was elevated and vascular resistance showed a slight decline while all indexes of cardiac function were in the direction of elevated activation. As in the aversive task, norepinephrine increased significantly from baseline, again indicating globally enhanced sympathetic activation. This pattern of cardiovascular and catecholamine change is similar to preparation for exercise. The results differed in one important respect, however. We saw no change in cortisol secretion from baseline. Subjective reports showed that the task was primarily activating and nonaversive, as we expected.

We interpreted these results as showing that activation of attentional and motor response centers in the brain can lead to substantial activation of cardiovascular function even in the absence of significant muscular activity. The lack of increase in cortisol we interpreted as being due to the nonaversive nature of the task.

■ Activation and Distress

The cardiovascular activation patterns in the examples in Figure 5.1 are similar to the patterns occurring during preparation for exercise and for fight or flight. Both tasks require significant mental effort, including heightened attention, and preparation for the execution of a motor plan, resulting in activation of motor areas of the cortex. These behavioral requirements presumably generate strong central commands that engage lower autonomic control centers, resulting in exercise-like cardiovascular adjustments even in the absence of actual exercise.

The strong similarities between the cardiovascular patterns in the two studies indicate that these were associated with the mental effort expended and the similar response requirements of both tasks. Both tasks evoked self-reports of significant concentration, effort, and activation, suggesting that the subjects were actively engaged in the effort of performing as well as possible regardless of the nature of the incentives. This effortful aspect of the tasks therefore seems most closely tied to the cardiovascular changes.

In contrast to these similarities between cardiovascular activation patterns, the cortisol responses were different in the two studies. Cortisol increased during the aversive task in relation to its perceived aversiveness but did not change in the rewarded task, as shown in Figure 5.2. This suggests that cortisol rises are evoked preferentially by feelings of distress associated with aversive circumstances and are not tied to expenditure of mental effort or to the specific behavioral demands of the tasks. For this reason, I liken the response to the rewarded task to exercise preparation and I have compared the response to the aversive task to a fight-flight response.

▨ Discussion

Substantial changes can occur in peripheral physiology because of mental activity. Preparation for physical exercise or performing a psychomotor task in the laboratory can invoke activational changes in cardiovascular function. These changes can occur regardless of the positive or negative emotions involved.

The cardiovascular response pattern documented to the reaction time task is not necessarily the same as the pattern seen with other mental stressors. For example, mental arithmetic produces increased heart rate and cardiac output elevations, but it does not result in the same reduction in peripheral resistance that one sees to reaction time (Allen et al., 1987). I suspect that this difference between the tasks in peripheral blood flow regulation has to do with differences in behavioral requirements. Mental arithmetic primarily engages working memory and does not involve intense preparation for motor activity, although the responses are usually spoken aloud. One may say, therefore, that the pattern of cardiovascular adjustment seen during a mentally challenging task depends on the degree of activation or mental effort the person exerts and on the behavioral characteristics of the task itself.

The second major point is that the emotional component of a task can determine the pattern of endocrine changes, especially the cortisol response. Cortisol can show a prompt and substantial increase in the bloodstream following the onset of potent aversive events such as electric shock. I have noted that the amount of cortisol rise is positively correlated with the negative perceptions of the subjects being tested.

These considerations lead one to recognize that not all increases in physiological activity from the resting level are signs of distress, and not all such increases signal unhealthy processes. Sometimes these changes are signs of activation in the absence of negative emotions. This distinction between

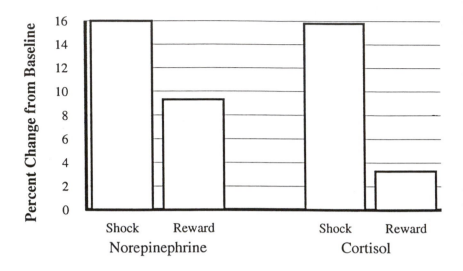

Figure 5.2. Neuroendocrine responses to reaction time tasks having aversive or monetary incentives.

activating and distressing events may be useful for thinking about the influence of mental stress on disease. First, exercise is a health-promoting, beneficial activity accompanied by positive emotional states. Second, fight-flight responses occurring in nature may differ from the evocation of these primitive reflexes in contemporary life. Charvat, Dell, and Folkow (1964) discuss possible differences in physiological changes associated with normal fight-flight reactions that develop rapidly, involve release in exercise, and are terminated when the encounter ends. In modern social settings, aggressive impulses are inhibited and hostile encounters rarely occur, and this may cause prolonged emotional and preparatory changes with no behavioral release. Charvat et al. argue that prolonged centrally generated activation may cause physiological changes associated with increased risk of disease. I have shown that the cortisol response may be a distinguishing feature of distressing events.

In Chapter 6, I will consider how challenges encountered in daily life can produce psychological stress responses and I will examine models of the resulting central nervous system functions leading to autonomic and pituitary adrenocortical activation.

SUMMARY

Humans have evolved a complex set of physiological controls to maintain homeostasis. These controls compensate for physical changes in the composition of the external or internal environment. In contrast to physical threats to homeostasis, we can often experience perceived threats and emotional upsets associated with psychological distress. Psychological stressors also affect the state of the body by altering the same mechanisms that we evolved to compensate for physical threats. I have discussed exercise as a typical example of physical stress and I have described psychomotor tasks and mental arithmetic as examples of psychological stressors commonly used in laboratory research. The emotional characteristics of these stressors are crucial for determining the pattern of autonomic and endocrine activation. Emotionally positive, activating challenges call forth increased cardiovascular and catecholamine responses without activating cortisol. Emotionally negative, distressed states selectively produce rises in cortisol to accompany the cardiovascular and catecholamine activation. Therefore, cortisol may be specifically sensitive to negative emotional states such as fear. The significance of psychological stress responses is that they are internally generated and affect the body in a top-down fashion. Such responses, often associated with negative emotions, may occur frequently in social settings without being acted out behaviorally. These repeated responses may have negative health consequences.

FURTHER READING

Charvat, J., Dell, P., & Folkow, B. (1964). Mental factors and cardiovascular diseases. *Cardiologia, 44,* 124-141.

This is a classic account of the theory that stress can lead to illness.

FitzGerald, M. J. T. (1992). *Neuroanatomy: Basic and clinical.* London: Ballière Tindall.

This is a useful review of neuroanatomy and its relation to functional brain systems.

Folkow, B. (1993). Physiological organization of neurohormonal responses to psychosocial stimuli. Implications for health and disease. *Annals of Behavioral Medicine, 15,* 236-244.

This is a recent account of integrated stress mechanisms in relation to behavior.

Guyton, A. C. (1992). *Human physiology and mechanisms of disease* (3rd ed.). Philadelphia: Saunders.

This is an excellent, comprehensive review of human physiology.

Rushmer, R. M. (1989). Structure and function of the cardiovascular system. In N. Schneiderman, P. Kaufmann, & S. Weiss (Eds.), *Handbook of research methods in cardiovascular behavioral medicine* (pp. 5-22). New York: Plenum.

This provides a brief overview of the structure and function of the cardiovascular system.

Stanford, S. C., & Salmon, P. (Eds.). (1993). *Stress: From synapse to syndrome.* New York: Academic Press.

This recent book provides a broad coverage of the field of stress.

Weiner, H. (1992). *Perturbing the organism: The biology of stressful experience.* Chicago: University of Chicago Press.

This provides a broad coverage of the field of stress.

Central Nervous System Integration of the Psychological Stress Response

In this chapter, I consider how a person's view of the world can influence his or her emotions and thereby cause psychological stress responses. To do so, I consider psychological stress as a set of functional interactions between the person and events in the environment. I next describe these same interactions using a neurophysiologically based model. Finally, I examine the neuroendocrine basis for the production of stress-related hormones. I therefore view the process of psychological stress using both functional and neurophysiological models in parallel to understanding how psychological responses are tied to events in the brain. This discussion will provide background for my basic question about the ways ideas can affect the body.

▓ Psychological Stress

Lazarus and Folkman (1984) describe how interactions with the environment generate emotions and how these can produce bodily stress responses. They note that we constantly evaluate the stream of events we encounter. In this appraisal process, we classify events as familiar or unfamiliar and threatening or nonthreatening. Similarly, we generate a stream of behavioral strategies to deal with these unfolding events. Along with these appraisals and behavioral adjustments, we experience emotions that signal us about the success of our behavioral strategies and motivate additional behaviors.

Primary and Secondary Appraisals

Lazarus and Folkman's (1984) model of psychological stress takes a cognitive view of how we engage the world. They postulate that we first evaluate events for their threat value. This primary appraisal is intended to ensure that we do not blindly encounter danger, but instead recognize it and begin to evolve a plan to deal with it. We next evaluate our options for coping with these presumed threats using secondary appraisals. This two-level appraisal process determines not only our cognitive and behavioral responses but also our emotional, neurophysiological, autonomic, and endocrine responses to external events. In short, our appraisals determine the nature and magnitude of our psychological reactions and their accompanying physiological adjustments. Figure 6.1 is a diagram of this appraisal-based model.

Lazarus and Folkman (1984) consider the main elements entering into our primary appraisal of an event to be our beliefs about how the world should work and our commitment to given courses of action. Events are judged to be benign or irrelevant or to be threats or challenges. Events are appraised as threatening if they violate our beliefs about the world or block our ability to carry out our commitments in life. Benign events are safely ignored, requiring no special adaptive response. When an event is considered a genuine threat, we have a simultaneous emotional reaction that signals alarm and motivates further behavioral and psychological responses along with physiological activation. We then evaluate the variety and availability of coping responses and their effectiveness at reducing or removing the threat.

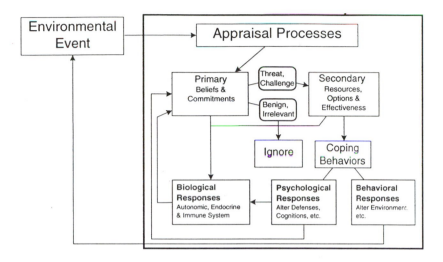

Figure 6.1. Model of psychological stress. The process of psychological stress includes both primary appraisals of the threat value of an event and secondary appraisals of the effectiveness of available coping options. These two processes have an effect on physiological responses to the situation. (Adapted from Lazarus & Folkman, 1984.)

The use of beliefs and commitments as the criteria for deciding what events are threatening provides a means of accounting for differences between individuals in how threatening an event may be. For example, if I fall and break my arm, I might find this event to be inconvenient, painful, and a disruption to my life. It is not something I would volunteer for, but I doubt that the misfortune would amount to a personal disaster. On the other hand, imagine this same broken arm happening to an athlete preparing to take part in the Olympic games. In this instance, the broken arm poses a serious threat to the athlete's commitment to a major goal in life. The otherwise manageable inconvenience of wearing a cast for several weeks turns into a devastating event: The athlete has to stop training and may have a severe psychological response such as depression. Clearly, the same event has different meanings for me and for the athlete because of differences in our personal commitments.

Coping Responses

The process of secondary appraisal focuses on the kinds of responses that might be employed to manage the event in question; again, people are likely to differ. Potential or known threats require some adaptive behavioral intervention to ensure that harm is avoided or its negative effects are limited. The interventions we employ are referred to as *coping strategies* and *coping behaviors*. These can include both overt and covert activities. If we find ourselves feeling chilly on a winter evening, obvious coping behaviors are to put on a sweater or to turn up the thermostat. Other situations in life are not so obviously correctable, and indeed no simple behavioral strategy may present itself. For example, parents confronted by the news that a young child has a serious, potentially life-threatening illness are likely to receive this as a devastating negative event—one that could have a serious effect on the child and threaten the integrity of the family. This news clearly violates both the beliefs and the commitments the parents share. The most appropriate responses to the situation are difficult to determine because of the complex questions at hand: Is the illness curable? What is the effect of the treatment on the child? How long will they have to confront this situation? Will there be financial burdens that may affect other children in the family? How will they manage the added time and energy demands possibly imposed by the situation? There are many potential responses, and all have their costs, strengths, and weaknesses.

In such a complex event as a major illness, the parents may use a multilevel strategy to limit the negative effect on themselves and the rest of the family. Such responses may include learning about the disease to assure that everything possible is being done for their child and altering their goals and expectations about the course of the child's development and the life of the family. These responses illustrate a combination of adaptive adjustments. Other parents might find themselves overwhelmed by the news and incapable of any directly adaptive response. Instead, they might deny that anything is wrong, insisting that the diagnosis is a mistake, even avoiding further treatment for the child. Responses to such a major life stressor may therefore involve cognitive approaches to the situation, behavioral adjustments, re-alignment of goals and commitments, or purely psychological approaches such as denial.

Lazarus and Folkman (1984) classify coping responses as *problem focused* and *emotion focused*. Problem-focused strategies attack the problem itself, with behaviors designed to gain information, to alter the event, and to alter beliefs and commitments. Problem-focused strategies increase the person's awareness, level of knowledge, and range of behavioral and cognitive coping options. They can act to reduce the threat value of the event. Emotion-focused strategies call for psychological changes designed primarily to limit the degree of emotional disruption caused by an event, with minimal effort to alter the event itself.

Outcomes of Coping Efforts and Physiological Responses

As might be expected, each coping strategy has its costs and benefits. Problem-focused strategies may be costly in terms of the energy and time necessary to put them into effect, but they can potentially lessen the stressor value of the event. Emotion-focused strategies are initially less energy consuming, but in the long term may be more costly due to a continued drain on coping resources. Whichever style of coping is employed, we strive to reduce the central nervous system activation associated with emotions and to reduce the physiological activation that ensues.

Once a coping strategy has been used, we again evaluate the event vis-à-vis our, perhaps new, beliefs and commitments and we reassess its threat value. Therefore, the appraisal process is recurrent, and our responses are continuously modified as we deal with the emerging challenges of life. An ultimate goal of the process is to reduce the threat value of events in the environment, to reduce the negative emotions in response to them, and therefore to reduce the inner state associated with stress reactions.

In the discussion of fight-flight responses in Chapter 5, I noted that these primitive behaviors are designed to aid our survival in a physically hostile environment. When we encounter events that threaten our beliefs and commitments, however, we may well find that we experience negative emotions and fight-flight responses even when our physical well-being is not at stake. Emotional reactions and physiological responses can result from our perception of threat from the environment and our perception of the success of our coping efforts.

Stress responses based on perceptions of threat are considered to be *psychological stress responses* because the threat value depends largely on our interpretation of the event and its meaning for our own lives. One might say the following things about psychological stressors:

1. They achieve their threat value not through their physical ability to do harm but because of their appraised threat value.
2. They are not equally stressful to all persons.
3. Persons will vary in their ability to cope with perceived stressors.
4. The physiological systems we use to respond to psychological stressors are the same ones that we use to react to physical threats to homeostasis.

Reflecting on the examples of psychological stress in Chapter 5, one notes that some stressors are pure examples of psychologically threatening events. When considering physically threatening events, however, one notes that these nearly always present a psychological threat as well in conscious persons. Being caught without shelter in a snowstorm will surely challenge the person's homeostatic mechanisms of temperature regulation, but the person is also likely to suffer considerable anxiety and emotional distress due to his or her awareness of the danger to his or her well-being. So one might say that persons conscious of their situation are likely to have significant psychological concomitants with any physical threat.

Lazarus and Folkman (1984) pose their model in cognitive terms, as though each event we encounter during the day is thought over and each response is selected consciously from a range of options. The model works equally well if the language of cognition is exchanged for the language of conditioning. One could assume that primary appraisals include implicit appraisals enacted via conditioned responses developed through prior experience. Similarly, one could think of secondary appraisals as being shaped by the enactment of behaviorally conditioned coping strategies from experience. Appraisals may therefore be relatively automatic, conditioned responses or they may be highly cognitive, planned ones.

In this discussion of appraisals and psychological stress, I place much emphasis on the generation of emotions as a result of the nature of the appraisals. It is likely that the particular emotion that results from a situation will depend heavily on the specifics of the appraisal process. Lazarus (1991, pp. 89-170) describes this relationship at some length.

In addition, the Lazarus and Folkman (1984) model does not specify how these processes might link up with central nervous system processes and peripheral outflow. Nevertheless, it is possible to specify plausible neurophysiological mechanisms for three major stages in this model of psychological stress: the primary appraisal process, the accompanying emotions and physiological responses, and modulation of these by coping responses.

▓ Central Integration of the Response to Psychological Stress

I now turn attention to a model illustrating how encounters with threatening events are incorporated into neurophysiological changes and autonomic and endocrine outflow. Figure 6.2 is a greatly simplified flow diagram of the chain of psychophysiological events that lead from an event in the environment to the generation of a bodily response. Five major steps make up this process:

1. Sensory intake and interpretation of the environment
2. Generation of emotions based on the appraisal processes
3. Initiation of autonomic and endocrine responses
4. Feedback to the cortex and limbic system
5. Autonomic and endocrine outflow

I will review these steps in detail referring to Figure 6.3, which refers to specific brain areas.

Sensory Inputs

Sensory information is relayed through the thalamus, which acts as the central way station for most incoming information. The thalamus directs information to the primary cortical projection areas dedicated to the various sensory modalities (designated 1 through n). This incoming information is passed through a series of cortical sensory association areas (designated a1 through a3), during which time raw sensory information is increasingly elaborated with stored information relating to that sensory modality. The endpoint for the input side of this model is the prefrontal cortex (designated the orbital and frontal pole). It is here that we attach meaning or significance to the information we receive. It is also at this point that information from the various modalities is integrated into a unified whole to provide an accurate picture of the external world. The evaluation of events as to meaning and significance captures the essence of the appraisal process.

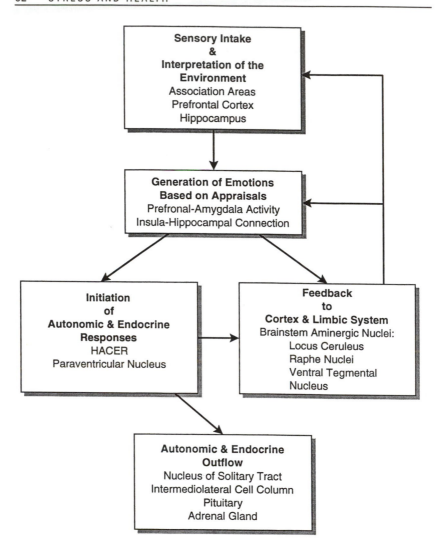

Figure 6.2. Major steps in the generation of physiological responses based on perceptions and interpretations of events.

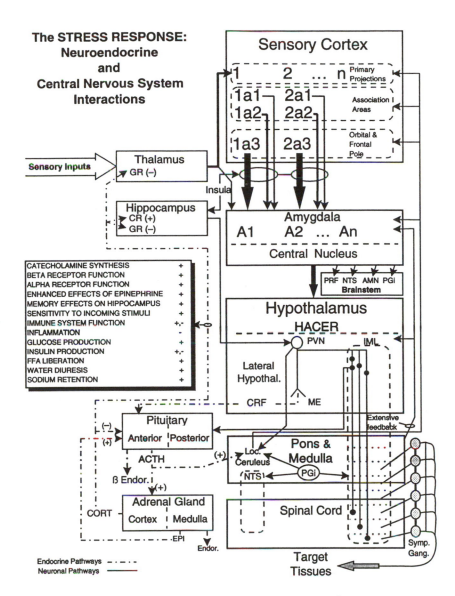

Figure 6.3. Neurophysiologically based model of the primary brain processes determining autonomic and endocrine responses to psychological stress.

Evaluating External Events and the
Consequences of Our Actions

There is much evidence that the frontal lobes, especially the prefrontal cortex, are essential for evaluating events, giving them meaning, and considering possible consequences of our actions. Recent work also suggests that these areas may participate in working memory. One might think of working memory as a process by which present events are consciously evaluated and courses of action are developed, just the sort of skills necessary to carry out primary and secondary appraisals.

Impressive demonstration of the role of the frontal lobes comes from patients who have sustained damage to these areas. Such persons find it difficult to invest events with meaning and to make informed choices about future actions based on feelings about their consequences. Much of this work is summarized engagingly by Damasio (1994), who reports that patients with frontal lesions are often fully conscious and able to perform normally on tests of intelligence. If asked to choose a course of action from several options, these patients may rationally discuss the pros and cons of each alternative, but they are unable to come down firmly in favor of one choice of action or the other, as if they cannot place value on the potential effects of their own actions.

Damasio (1994) provides the striking example of a patient with frontal damage who was given a simple choice of two dates for a follow-up appointment about a month later. Most persons would think for a moment and state a preference for one option. In this case, the patient began a lengthy discussion of each option, rationally stating the pros and cons of each, but in spite of this evaluation, he was unable to decide which date would be better until his physician, in desperation, suggested a date. The patient immediately agreed to that date and happily left the office as though all his former discussion was irrelevant! In Damasio's words,

> We might conclude that the result of these patients' lesions is the discarding of what their brains have acquired through education and socialization. One of the most distinctive human traits is the ability to learn to be guided by future prospects rather than by immediate outcomes. (p. 218)

Damasio thus considers the importance of the frontal lobes and their connections to limbic structures in the temporal and frontal lobes to be their ability to invest information with meaning and emotional valence, to look toward the consequences of a course of action, allowing us to warm up to one alternative and to act on that decision. These prefrontal-limbic connections act to help us feel about things, not just to compare sterile bits of information coldly. This reasoning leads one to place the frontal cortex at the beginning of the chain of events resulting in normal emotional responses and perhaps leading to physiological stress responses. I should also note that the patients described by Damasio are not necessarily devoid of emotional experience. Such patients can have spontaneous bursts of emotion at inappropriate times. What these patients lack is the ability to have normal emotional responses in relation to present thoughts and events. For this reason, I speak of emotions formed in response to environmental events as arising from a transaction between the prefrontal areas and the hippocampus and amygdala located in the temporal lobe.

Physiological Correlates of Primary and Secondary Appraisal Processes

Returning for a moment to the model of psychological stress responses, I see a strong parallel between primary appraisals and the functions of the frontal lobe that allow us to give meaning to events. During secondary appraisals, we must be able to invest alternative coping strategies with both meaning and emotional content to choose, we hope, the best alternative. The addition of emotional content appears to depend on connecting the activity of the prefrontal cortex with other structures specialized for the formation of emotional responses. Both steps in the appraisal process involve activity of the limbic system, including the amygdala and hippocampus, accompanied by the insular cortex.

The limbic system is intimately connected to the incoming flow of sensory information, but it can also take control of autonomic centers in the hypothalamus and brainstem when response to external events is required. In Figure 6.3, the primary limbic system structures are the amygdala and hippocampus.

The connections between the frontal cortex and amygdala are indicated by a series of arrows. The thickness of the arrows shows that the highly elaborated information from prefrontal areas is also more heavily represented to the amygdala. In addition, the hippocampus receives information about the traffic moving from the frontal cortex to the amygdala by way of the insular cortex, indicated in the figure as a two-headed arrow and labeled simply as *Insula*. The hippocampus is involved in memory storage and in putting new information together with prior experience. The hippocampus and surrounding cortex are critical for the operation of declarative memory, our ability to recall specific events as opposed to abstract factual information. In this sense, the hippocampus also plays a crucial role in evaluating the stream of continuing experience.

Equally important is the amygdala, which is critical in enabling us to have emotions in connection with present experience and to modify our actions based on those emotions and knowledge of the past. The insular cortex is essential for allowing the prefrontal cortex and amygdala to carry on their experiential-emotional dialogue.

Research using animal models has indicated the importance of the amygdala in generating appropriate responses to threatening situations. In Chapter 5, I noted that behavioral avoidance and stress-related endocrine responses were observed by Brady (1955) in his studies of primates exposed to novel, potentially threatening, events. Surgically amygdalectomized animals do not hesitate to approach and explore unfamiliar objects, however. Similarly, the amygdala is important for matching environmental cues with negative emotions such as disgust, fear, or anger. Amygdalectomized animals are very slow to learn to avoid places where aversive stimulation has occurred or to learn to escape when given cues signaling impending shock. Another way to look at these results is that amygdalectomized animals are deprived of their ability to look forward to potential negative consequences of their behaviors in light of current sensory information. This interpretation is supported by the experience of humans who report fear in response to electrical stimulation of the amygdala. A detailed discussion is provided by LeDoux (1993).

The processes served by the amygdala, hippocampus, and insular cortex are critical for both primary and secondary appraisals as outlined in Lazarus and Folkman's (1984) model of psychological stress. Primary appraisals involve recognizing if something is dangerous. Secondary appraisals involve reviewing the available coping responses, evaluating a plan of action, and examining possible outcomes in view of their costs and benefits. The frontal-limbic connections specified in Figure 6.3 suggest that the psychological processes postulated by Folkman and Lazarus have known neurophysiological counterparts.

Figure 6.3 also indicates a direct connection from the thalamus to the amygdala, bypassing the sensory and association cortexes. This direct path is thought to serve as an early warning system, allowing very rapid, global avoidance and defense responses that might not occur rapidly enough if they followed the more elaborate, and necessarily slower, processing indicated by the usual route.

Sources of Amygdaloid Activity and Internally Generated Emotional Responses

I have spoken of psychological stressors as though they always begin as external events. But some of the most consistent sources of psychological distress are our own thoughts and ruminations. Schulkin, McEwen, and Gold (1994) describe how we may agonize over future events or past actions and how such mental activity may generate the same responses of the frontal lobes and the amygdala that would occur if we were confronting a genuine threat. These recalled or imagined events are certainly able to engage the limbic system.

Understanding the frontal and limbic mechanisms underlying the generation of emotions helps us appreciate the very close association we have between our evaluation of the world, our formulations of coping strategies, and our emotional experience.

Formulation of Behavioral, Autonomic, and Neuroendocrine Responses to Psychological Stressors

The next critical step in the model of the biology of psychological stress is to consider how appraisals and emotions lead to changes in our peripheral physiology by way of autonomic and endocrine outputs.

The basal and lateral areas of the amygdala are shown in Figure 6.3 as receiving information from frontal areas in terms of specific modalities (indicated as A1, A2, etc.). In turn, the medial and central areas of the amygdala send outputs to the hypothalamus and brainstem via the central nucleus. Consider the relationship of the amygdala to frontal areas and the limbic system and its very large neural output to the hypothalamus and brainstem. These relationships lead us to consider the amygdala as a focal point of transition between sensory input and interpretations of the world on the one hand and our formulation of autonomic and endocrine responses on the other.

The connections from the central nucleus of the amygdala to the brainstem include the following targets: the pontine reticular formation (PRF), the nucleus of the solitary tract (NTS), the nucleus paragigantocellularis (PGi), and the brainstem aminergic nuclei (AMN). The outputs are shown immediately below the amygdala for visual clarity. The target structures are also represented in their actual brainstem locations in the pons and medulla.

These brainstem regions form two functional subsystems. The first is the central feedback subsystem, which includes the pontine reticular formation and its aminergic nuclei. This subsystem serves to alter the functional state of the entire central nervous system, causing it to switch gears to meet behavioral emergencies and to become quiescent when appropriate. The second subsystem is the brainstem response subsystem, which includes the nucleus paragigantocellularis, the nucleus of the solitary tract, and the intermediolateral cell column. This subsystem modulates the autonomic responses that descend to the vital organs and skeletal muscles as required by the situation.

Central Feedback Subsystem

The central feedback subsystem consists of the reticular formation and its more specialized components, especially the aminergic nuclei. This subsystem determines the global behavioral state of the person. Depending on commands from the amygdala and hypothalamus, it can prepare us to meet an emergency if we need to respond to one, or it can put us to sleep if it is safe to do so.

The PRF is a diffuse collection of fibers and specialized nuclei. It is phylogenetically very old. In primitive species, it connects sensory systems with systems allowing the formation of behavioral and physiological responses. It plays a similar role in humans, with considerably greater integration with and control from higher centers, especially motor and decision making systems controlled by the cortex.

The AMN contain cell bodies that synthesize the monoamine neurotransmitters: norepinephrine, serotonin, and dopamine. The locus ceruleus contains 90% of the norepinephrine-synthesizing cell bodies in the central nervous system. The raphe nuclei in turn synthesize most of the serotonin.

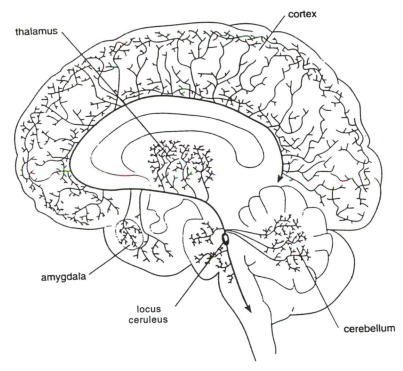

Figure 6.4. The projections of noradrenergic fibers from the locus ceruleus to the rest of the central nervous system.

Both sets of nuclei send their aminergic fibers to the cortex, limbic structures, and spinal cord. These small groupings of cell bodies are therefore extremely important in determining the state of the entire cortex and in shaping the interplay of emotional experience, brain states, and autonomic and motor outflow. The extent of the connections from the locus ceruleus to the rest of the central nervous system is indicated in Figure 6.4 (see Aston-Jones, Ennis, Pieribone, Nickell, & Shipley, 1986).

Because the AMN receive abundant inputs directly or indirectly from the amygdala, one might expect that they are sensitive to negative mood states. This is the case. For example, reduced norepinephrine in the locus ceruleus has been implicated in animal models of depression. Similarly reduced function of the raphe nuclei shown by low serotonin levels is associated with defective social interactions and increased hostility and violent behavior (Brown, Goodwin, Ballenger, Goyer, & Major, 1986). I say more about the locus ceruleus and raphe nuclei in Chapter 7, but one can see that the amygdala, acting directly on these nuclei, can alter the functional state of the central nervous system and organize responses appropriate to such negative moods.

I note in passing that the dopaminergic fibers project upward from the ventral tegmental area, above the pons, to the cortex. They seem to modulate the processing of incoming information, and altered dopaminergic function is implicated in the symptoms of schizophrenia. The dopaminergic system, in conjunction with the serotonergic system, is also thought to generate the experience of pleasure associated with reward, again indicating its effect on processing of incoming information and its effects on mood and hedonic aspects of our experience (see Blum, Cull, Braverman, & Comings, 1996).

The central feedback subsystems associated with the brainstem AMN therefore serve to coordinate the level of arousal and behavioral state of the entire central nervous system in response to the commands of the amygdala or other limbic structures. These are very primitive systems, but one can think of them as coordinating the entire system whether the situation calls for fight-flight, approach, avoidance, or sleep.

Brainstem Response Subsystem

The amygdala also sends fibers to the nucleus of the solitary tract, NTS, in Figure 6.3. This nucleus is important in organizing cardiovascular reflexes, especially baroreceptor feedback and blood pressure regulation. The action of the amygdala appears to be responsible for inhibition of the baroreceptor reflex during states of stress, as described in Chapter 4. This descending influence is a good example of how the amygdala can modulate homeostatic reflexes that would otherwise attend only to internal states of the body.

Finally, the amygdala also communicates with the nucleus paragiganto-cellularis, shown as PGi. This nucleus is important for skeletal motor reflex pattern generation. It is closely associated with the locus ceruleus, the nucleus of the solitary tract, and the intermediolateral cell column. As I note in Chapter 4, the intermediolateral cell column runs from the hypothalamus, through the pons and medulla, down into the spinal cord, and carries the fibers that communicate with the sympathetic preganglionic fibers. Again, one can see that the amygdala is able to monitor activity in the prefrontal cortex and then exert control over autonomic reflexes and skeletal motor function via its connections to the pons and medulla.

Hypothalamic Activation During Stress

The other major target of amygdaloid output is the hypothalamus, or more specifically, an area referred to by Smith and colleagues (Smith et al., 1993; Smith, DeVito, & Astley, 1982) as the *HACER* (the Hypothalamic Area Controlling Emotional Responses, pronounced ah-SEHR). Studies in rats and primates have shown that autonomic responses to aversive events, including threat of capture or electric shock, are absent when the areas corresponding to the HACER have been destroyed. The behavioral correlates of threat, however, such as muscular tensing and facial grimacing, are present, indicating that the animal is aware of the impending threat and is experiencing the event appropriately. What appears to be missing are important links to physiological outputs to the periphery. In such animals, the usual cardiovascular changes associated with such threats are greatly diminished. The term HACER is used in favor of more traditional anatomical designations because several hypothalamic nuclei are involved, and the collection does not correspond directly to a single anatomical designation.

Activation of the HACER Leads to Neuroendocrine
and Autonomic Outputs From the Hypothalamus

The endocrine and autonomic outputs from the hypothalamus are shown in greatly simplified form in Figure 6.3. First, endocrine changes result from activation of the paraventricular nucleus (PVN) of the hypothalamus, causing secretion of corticotropin releasing factor (CRF) from the median eminence (ME). CRF causes secretion of β endorphin and adrenocorticotropin (ACTH) by the anterior pituitary and then secretion of cortisol by the adrenal cortex. Cortisol in turn has widespread effects in the periphery; these are listed in the box on the left side of Figure 6.3.

Cortisol also has an important feedback role at several places in the central nervous system. I noted in Chapter 4 that normal secretion of cortisol relies on tonic activity of the hippocampus. The hippocampus is the primary site of circulating cortisol's negative feedback responsible for regulation of its secretion over the diurnal cycle. Cortisol also exerts negative feedback at the hypothalamus to regulate ACTH and CRF secretion. At the hippocampus, and thalamus, cortisol acts on two types of receptors: cortisol receptors (CR) and glucocorticoid receptors (GR). GRs appear to be sensitive to low levels of cortisol and to be responsible for modulating hippocampal activation over the diurnal cycle. CRs appear to be sensitive only to higher levels of cortisol and to enhance hippocampal activation. These are discussed in the next section as part of the description of the central nervous system CRF system. The CRF system integrates the central nervous system's response to aversive events and negative emotions.

The second major set of hypothalamic outputs in response to activation of the HACER are fibers going from the PVN to the brainstem that modulate autonomic function. These fibers travel to the locus ceruleus, intermediolateral cell column, and nucleus paragigantocellularis. As a result, they affect the magnitude of sympathetic outflow to the peripheral tissues. Therefore, the hypothalamus, by secreting CRF to the pituitary and by sending neuronal fibers to the brainstem, coordinates the autonomic and endocrine arms of the stress response. Recent work shows that the primary integration of output signals to the cardiovascular and endocrine components of the fight-flight response is through the paraventricular nucleus of the hypothalamus (Jansen, Nguyen, Karpitskiy, Mettenleiter, & Loewy, 1995).

A final point on response integration concerns epinephrine secretion. Increased sympathetic activity causes secretion of epinephrine from the adrenal medulla. Epinephrine, in turn, can stimulate ACTH secretion by the pituitary, therefore coordinating the two major arms of the hormonal response to stress, the hypothalamic-sympatho-adrenomedullary system and the hypothalamic-pituitary-adrenocortical system.

Hierarchy of Autonomic and Endocrine Controls Over Homeostasis

In Chapter 4, I discussed the functional organization of the organs innervated by the autonomic nervous system. I noted that the entire system is characterized by functional autonomy on the part of individual organs and by modulatory influences and integration of function imposed by higher levels in the system, including the spinal cord, brainstem autonomic nuclei, and the hypothalamus. This functional organization also includes the limbic system and the cortex. Most autonomic and endocrine adaptations are functionally complete at the level of the hypothalamus. Reflex organization at this level permits full regulation of organic function and allows the system to respond in an appropriately coordinated fashion to departures from homeostasis.

If the system included only the hypothalamus and lower structures, however, the organism would lack the ability to make behavioral responses, such as finding food, or to respond to distant threats. The recognition of an aggressor requires that the aggressor be seen, felt, smelled, or heard. Such functions are the province of a sensory apparatus and a memory system, both associated with the cortex, and with specialized structures for interpreting these events and beginning to formulate a response. The limbic system, acting through the amygdala, is able to take command of the autonomic and endocrine control centers of the hypothalamus and brainstem when a threat is encountered. This temporarily redirects them from their metabolic and homeostatic chores to devote their resources to support the behaviors needed to meet the emergency. Thus, the cortex and limbic system represent the highest levels of control in the nervous system, able to supersede, if only briefly, the usual physiological business of maintaining homeostasis.

Based on this analysis, one can see that homeostasis is served by an elaborate hierarchy of controls, starting with intrinsic organ regulation, through the brainstem and hypothalamus, to cortical and limbic areas, and through them to behavior. Felten and coworkers (Felten et al., 1991) have shown that behaviors that restore homeostasis are rewarded, presumably by alteration of limbic system activity. This again argues for a strong linkage among emotions, behavior, and control over our internal states. I note above that during psychological stress, coping behaviors, whether problem focused or emotion focused, work to reduce the emotional agitation associated with limbic activity. This reduction appears to act as a reward, and therefore long-term behavioral tendencies can act to contribute to the improved maintenance of homeostasis.

▓ The Central Nervous CRF System

The analysis of the brain's ability to organize the body's responses to psychological stressors would not be complete without taking a second, more detailed look at the brain's internal organization of the emotional, cognitive, behavioral, and physiological components of the stress response. This organization depends heavily on the role of CRF. Historically, CRF was identified as the neuropeptide responsible for activation of the hypothalamic-pituitary-adrenocortical axis (HPAC). At the ME of the hypothalamus, CRF terminals were found to interface with the portal circulation, carrying CRF down the pituitary stalk to the anterior pituitary. Here CRF binds to receptors on corticotroph cells, which then release ACTH into the systemic circulation. ACTH in turn increases the rate of production of cortisol by the cortex of the adrenal gland. CRF and ACTH both vary over the diurnal cycle and in response to stressors. CRF is therefore recognized as playing a central role in regulating cortisol secretion over the diurnal cycle and in response to metabolic demands.

More recent evidence shows that CRF also acts as a neurotransmitter in a widespread system of neurons that appears to integrate sensory information with emotion, behavior, and autonomic and hormonal response systems. The functions of the corticotropin system appear to be very old. The CRF gene is highly conserved across species from annelid worms to mammals. Expression of the CRF gene is inhibited by cortisol. The CRF neuron system of the central nervous system is shown in Figure 6.5. Figure 6.5 relates closely to Figure 6.3, although the two differ in their detail concerning frontal-limbic connections and neuroendocrine controls.

Distribution of CRF-Containing Cell Bodies

The greatest single accumulation of neurons with CRF-producing cell bodies is found in the paraventricular nucleus (PVN) of the hypothalamus. Some of these cells project to the ME of the hypothalamus and others to the brainstem and the spinal cord. Other major accumulations of CRF cell bodies are found in the prefrontal, insular, and cingulate cortexes and the hippocampus. It appears that the CRF-synthesizing neurons originating in these prefrontal and limbic areas are very important for integrating emotions into the central nervous system's formulation of behavioral and physiological stress responses. Figure 6.5 gives precedence to the CRF cell bodies of the central nucleus of the amygdala because these form primary outputs to the hypothalamus and brainstem from the integrated activity of the prefrontal cortex and limbic structures. These hypothalamic and brainstem connections have far-reaching consequences for integrating the central nervous system response to negative emotions and stress.

Autonomic Regulation and CRF Neurons

CRF-containing neurons project to and from several major centers involved in control of autonomic function: (1) the dense accumulation of

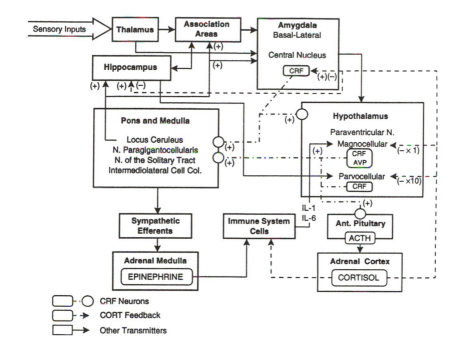

Figure 6.5. The central nervous system corticotropin releasing factor (CRF) system.

CRF cell bodies found in the central nucleus of the amygdala projects to the brainstem autonomic nuclei and to the PVN of the hypothalamus; (2) hypothalamic inputs to the autonomic nervous system contain CRF-synthesizing fibers arising from the PVN that project to the intermediolateral cell column and spinal cord; and (3) the brainstem contains significant concentrations of CRF-containing neurons around the locus ceruleus and nucleus paragigantocellularis, the nucleus of the solitary tract, and the autonomic control centers of the medulla. These project upstream to the cortex and limbic system and downstream to the spinal cord. Finally, in the spinal cord, CRF-containing neurons act as sympathetic preganglionic fibers. Considering this range of connections, the central CRF system appears to integrate the central nervous system's responses during stress-producing situations, especially those involving negative emotional states and states calling for fight and flight.

CRF Fibers and Pituitary-Autonomic Integration

The pituitary normally responds to diurnal cycles and metabolic demands in its regulation of cortisol secretion. This is controlled by the secretion of CRF at the ME in response to signals generated by the PVN. During psychological stress, however, the initiating signals to the PVN begin in the amygdala. The PVN contains two subsets of CRF neurons, known as parvocellular and magnocellular neurons, and these are differentially responsive to signals from the amygdala.

The parvocellular portion of the PVN contains CRF-synthesizing cell bodies responsive to normal homeostatic and diurnal variations. CRF production here is regulated by feedback of peripheral cortisol, and this regulation is accomplished through receptors that are highly sensitive to cortisol as indicated by the designation "–X 10" in Figure 6.5.

In contrast, the magnocellular portion of the PVN contains CRF neurons that also synthesize arginine vasopressin (AVP). Activation of these CRF-AVP synthesizing neurons produces a much larger release of ACTH by the pituitary, apparently due to a synergistic effect of CRF and AVP at the pituitary corticotrophs. These neurons are also less sensitive than CRF-only neurons to negative feedback by peripheral cortisol, thus lowering the usual negative feedback regulation on the hypothalamic-pituitary-adrenal axis (Dallman, 1993). The CRF-AVP subpopulation of neurons is also the one that projects to the brainstem regulatory centers, notably the locus ceruleus and intermediolateral cell column. Therefore, the CRF-AVP synthesizing cells of the magnocellular portion of the PVN are important in the integration of the final development of the autonomic and endocrine components of stress responses by the central nervous system. This population of magnocellular cells is only about 1/10 as responsive as the parvocellular cells to the negative feedback effects of peripheral cortisol, indicated by "–X 1" in Figure 6.5. Therefore, during acute stress, cortisol secretion is much less sensitive to negative feedback regulation by peripheral cortisol. This is partly due to the tenfold difference in the cortisol sensitivity of parvocellular and magnocellular CRF and CRF-AVP secreting neurons. It is also due to the effect of cortisol on the amygdala. Stress levels of cortisol act on the central nucleus of the amygdala to increase the activity of CRF-secreting neurons, therefore exerting an amplifying effect on the CRF system and cortisol secretion during stress.

This integration of central responses by CRF is complemented by the integration of peripheral responses through the adrenal gland. The adrenal gland integrates the parallel outflow of the brainstem-autonomic and hypothalamus-endocrine branches of the peripheral response to psychological distress. The adrenal medulla produces epinephrine via sympathetic activity and the adrenal cortex produces cortisol. The adrenal gland is the final common pathway for these two important arms of the peripheral endocrine response to stress.

Cortisol Has Dual Modes of Regulation

These differences in regulation between normal diurnal or homeostatic functions and stress-related secretion are consistent with Munck's (Munck et al., 1984) hypothesis that cortisol has two basic families of functions termed *permissive* and *regulatory*. The permissive functions serve normal homeostatic needs and are highly subject to regulation by negative feedback from peripheral cortisol. The regulatory functions primarily counterregulate other peripheral effects occurring during stress. The feedback systems of the central nervous system tolerate higher levels of circulating cortisol with less negative feedback to the hypothalamus, hippocampus, and thalamus. Because of the short duration of most stress responses and their emergency nature, it may be desirable for the system to be able to produce large quantities of cortisol unrestricted by negative feedback.

Epinephrine also acts to augment the large secretion of cortisol occurring during states of stress. As Chapter 5 notes, epinephrine is secreted in large quantities only during states of emotional distress and substantial metabolic need or to support significant sympathetically mediated functions such as exercise. At these times, epinephrine may act on the hypothalamus to increase the release of CRF, thus promoting the release of cortisol.

Endocrine-Immune Interactions

A final element in the discussion of central nervous system involvement in stress responses concerns the immune system. Infected cells in the body secrete endocrine messengers known as cytokines. At least two of these (interleukin-1 and interleukin-6) reach the hypothalamus and stimulate the magnocellular population of CRF-AVP synthesizing cells. This mechanism is responsible for the large increase in cortisol secretion during illness. This response also leads to cortisol's regulation of specific aspects of the immune system's functioning during stress. A more complete description of these endocrine-immune interactions is given in Chapter 8.

▓ The Formation of Psychological Stress Responses

In this chapter, I have described the mechanisms by which the brain organizes responses to meet homeostatic demands during stressful events. In previous chapters, I described the peripheral systems active in homeostasis and their expression of the response to some stressors. I also distinguished between physical and psychological stressors, and I indicated that responses to physical stressors, such as exercise, were also engaged during exposure to psychological stressors. In this chapter, I have given a more refined description of psychological stressors as involving cognitive or conditioned appraisals of the threat value of events and appraisals of the outcome of coping responses.

The critical juncture in understanding mechanisms of psychological stress is to consider how primary and secondary appraisals can come to be translated into physical events that influence the state of the body. I have given a partial answer here to the question about the relationship between psychological and physiological events. The frontal lobes, the site of working memory, interact with critical structures in the limbic system and respond in relation to prior experience with certain classes of events. Known or presumed threats are experienced in a way that generates negative emotional responses associated with patterns of interaction among the prefrontal cortex, the amygdala, the hippocampus, the septal area, and the insular cortex.

The central nucleus of the amygdala, addressing the HACER and the PVN of the hypothalamus, is seen as the primary output pathway from these rostral decision-making and evaluative processes and in the development of adaptive neuroendocrine and autonomic responses. The system of neurons integrating this response is the central nervous system CRF system. This system binds together the functions of the brainstem and hypothalamus, in turn causing integrated outflow to the periphery. The other important system is the brainstem aminergic neuronal system, especially the locus ceruleus and raphe nuclei because of their ability to activate the entire central nervous system in response to signals from the amygdala.

All the regulatory systems described here can come under the control of events that have primarily symbolic threat value, acting as psychological stressors, and that can be internally generated. These systems, designed to maintain homeostasis, are ultimately regulated by behavior and in turn shape behaviors according to the behavior's ability to reduce limbic activity associated with distress. McEwen and Stellar (1993) propose a model similar to the one presented here. Their model draws heavily on the concept of allostasis. *Allostasis* is defined by them as the compensation that an organism engages in to maintain homeostasis successfully in the face of a consistent, moderate stressor. The concept implies that levels of compensatory activity, although successful at maintaining homeostasis, ultimately result in damaging consequences due to the long-term physiological activation involved. Although the allostasis concept has not been explicitly used here, the idea that continued levels of compensatory activation can be harmful is the same.

One message of the foregoing description is that the brainstem nuclei receiving inputs from the amygdala not only produce widespread alterations in the magnitude and balance of autonomic outflow, they also provide important feedback to the entire cortex and limbic system, altering their state and level of activation. This reciprocal relationship between the amygdala and brainstem control nuclei would appear to be well suited to helping the system meet a threat. The descending influences, acting via the intermediolateral cell column, prepare the body for fight or flight. The ascending influences focus the attentional and affective response resources of the central nervous system to become fully aware of the danger and to adjust responses as needed.

SUMMARY

In this chapter, I have considered how our perceptions of the world and our perceptions of our ability to cope with challenges in our environment can become the basis for emotional states. Through a process of primary and secondary appraisals, we begin to formulate our physiological responses to psychologically stressful events. In Chapter 4, I described the layers of control we can use to maintain physiological homeostasis. We can use our higher cognitive functions, involving frontal areas of the cerebral cortex, to evaluate external events in conjunction with critical structures of the limbic system. These evaluative processes form the basis for emotions and for the formulation of behavioral, autonomic, and endocrine responses to threatening events. We may therefore think of these psychological processes as exerting the highest level of control over our homeostatic functions. More generally, we may think of the appraisal process and its effects on stress responses as being central to our basic question of how ideas can come to have power over our bodies.

FURTHER READING

Averill, J. R. (1973). Personal control over aversive stimuli and its relation to stress. *Psychological Bulletin, 80,* 286-303.

This provides brief discussion of predictability and control as moderators of stress.

Damasio, A. R. (1994). *Descartes' error: Emotion, reason, and the human brain.* New York: Putnam.

This book on reason and emotion is a rich account of the clinical consequences of frontal lobe damage and the importance of prefrontal areas for evaluative processes.

Lazarus, R. S. (1991). *Emotion and adaptation.* New York: Oxford University Press.

This presents an extensive update of Lazarus's views of emotion in relation to appraisals, coping processes, and adaptive behavior.

Lazarus, R. S., & Folkman, S. (1984). *Stress, appraisal and coping.* New York: Springer.

This presents a valuable, extended consideration of coping processes and psychological stress.

Smith, O. A., & DeVito, J. L. (1984). Central neural integration for the control of autonomic responses associated with emotion. *Annual Review of Neurosciences, 7,* 43-65.

This is a well-integrated account of the organization of higher influences on autonomic outflow in relation to the emotions.

Helplessness,
Coping, and Health

In Chapter 6, I presented Lazarus and Folkman's (1984) model of the psychological stress response. That model emphasizes perceived control over the environment as a critical determinant of the psychological effect of events. I will now discuss the physiological effects of extreme loss of control in animal and human studies. These form a basis for thinking about the more limited loss of control people are likely to encounter in daily life. I will consider two major brainstem systems that may mediate widespread influences of severe stress on emotions, sympathetic outflow, and health. These are the noradrenergic, locus ceruleus system and the serotonergic, raphe nuclei. Considering the effects of perceived loss of control will provide an added dimension to the basic question of how ideas can come to have power over the body.

■ **Death Due to
Uncontrollable Stress**

To emphasize the importance of controllability over events and the ability to master the environment, I begin by considering death, the most extreme result of psychological stress. In "Voodoo Death," Cannon (1957) recounts reports of persons dying because they believed someone had cast a spell on them and that they had no chance of surviving. In preliterate societies, persons are apt to believe that the world is inhabited by good and evil forces and that some persons have the ability to harness the evil forces to harm others. Cannon notes reports of the casting of spells and the victims' resulting extreme fear and hopelessness:

> Dr. Lambert . . . wrote to me concerning the experience of Dr. P. S. Clarke. . . . One day a Kanaka came to his hospital and told him he would die in a few days because a spell had been put upon him and nothing could be done to counteract it. The man had been known by Dr. Clarke for some time. He was given a very thorough examination, including an examination of the stool and the urine. All was found normal, but as he lay in bed he gradually grew weaker, Dr. Clarke called upon the foreman of the Kanakas to come to the hospital to give the man assurance, but on reaching the foot of the bed the foreman leaned over, looked at the patient, and then turned to Dr. Clarke saying, "Yes, doctor, close up him he die." . . . The next day, at 11 o'clock in the morning, he ceased to live. A postmortem examination [revealed] nothing that could in any way account for the fatal outcome. (pp. 183-184)

There are common characteristics to Cannon's (1957) instances of voodoo death. The victims believed in magic, that a specific fatal threat was present, and that no escape was possible. These steps are remarkably parallel to primary and secondary appraisals in my description of psychological stress in Chapter 6. The psychological origin of this form of death is strongly suggested by the rapid reversal of the process when the occasional victim was convinced that the spell had been lifted. Cannon speculates that the profound feelings of hopelessness engendered in the victims of voodoo death resulted in severe metabolic and autonomic imbalances, often accompanied by failure to take in nutrients, resulting in death within days to weeks.

Sudden Death Due to Uncontrollable Stress

The examples of voodoo death may sound exotic and out of touch with modern life. Nevertheless, there are numerous recent examples of sudden death precipitated by psychological causes. Engel (1971) did an extensive search of newspaper accounts of persons dying suddenly under extreme circumstances. In most cases, the victim experienced a personal loss, such as death of a spouse or child or separation from a loved one. Often the person had a restricted range of social contacts and experienced the loss as irreplaceable and severe. Still other persons were faced with an exceptionally difficult personal dilemma in which the available courses of action all led to undesirable outcomes. In other cases, a violently emotional confrontation, often involving the severing of strong personal ties, preceded the sudden death, whereas other persons had returned home to discover their houses had been burglarized and ransacked.

Certainly, the emotional content differed in the various incidents Engel (1971) reports. Nevertheless, the emotions were all powerful negative ones, including anger and fear, and death appeared to be preceded by overwhelming feelings of helplessness or hopelessness. In cases where medical information was available, the cause of death was most often attributable to massive myocardial infarction or cerebrovascular stroke.

Recent patient reports show that the likelihood of a heart attack is about two times greater than usual in the 2 hours following an episode of anger (Mittleman et al., 1995). Reports of sudden coronary death and stroke can rise substantially during times of increased threat to the population. During the Los Angeles earthquake of 1994, more than half of all immediate deaths were due to sudden cardiac death, not to injuries. Death records show that sudden coronary deaths were five times greater than expected on the day of the earthquake (Leor, Poole, & Kloner, 1996). During Operation Desert Storm in 1991, deaths rose dramatically in Israel during the Iraqi Scud missile attacks. In targeted cities, death rates due to heart attack and related causes were more than twice normal (Kark, Goldman, & Epstein, 1995).

Possible Mechanisms of Sudden Death

Figure 7.1 illustrates five major steps by which overwhelming uncontrollable threat can lead to sudden death:

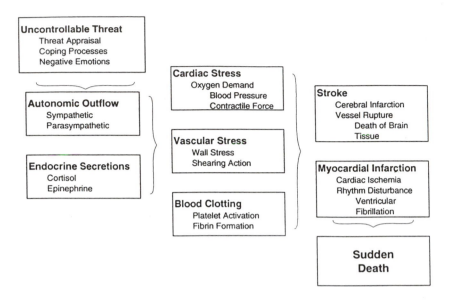

Figure 7.1. Events leading from uncontrollable psychological stress to sudden death.

1. Contact with an uncontrollable aversive event triggers primary threat appraisals, secondary appraisals that coping resources are limited, and negative emotions, as described in Figure 6.1.

2. Such emotions can significantly increase autonomic outflow to the peripheral organs and increase secretion of the stress-related hormones epinephrine and cortisol.

3. These autonomic and endocrine changes can increase the demand of the heart muscle for oxygen, increase stress on the walls of the blood vessels due to elevated blood pressure, and enhance the formation of blood clots.

4. Vascular stress, along with increased clotting, increases the risk of cerebrovascular stroke. Cardiac stress increases the risk of myocardial infarction and left ventricular arrhythmias leading to ventricular fibrillation.

5. Stroke, myocardial infarction, and ventricular arrhythmia are the most common causes of sudden death. The boxes in Figure 7.1 are not connected by arrows because the specific relationships among them are many.

Stress-induced fatal heart attacks or strokes occur most often in persons who already have atherosclerosis of the coronary arteries or arteriosclerosis of the arteries supplying the brain. The buildup of arterial plaque has several consequences:

1. The plaque narrows the vessel, resulting in episodes of ischemia (a lack of sufficient oxygen delivery to the tissues) when stress leads to increased oxygen demand.
2. The affected blood vessels are especially subject to the formation of blood clots, blocking the vessel and causing ischemia and possible myocardial infarction or stroke.
3. The plaque weakens the blood vessel wall, with the risk of arterial rupture, again leading to infarction or stroke. All these consequences of stress can result in ischemia and possible tissue damage.

Stress-induced arrhythmia of the heart can also result from ischemia and result in sudden cardiac death. Cardiac muscle ischemia during increased oxygen demand can lead to a loss of normal cardiac rhythm, resulting in ventricular tachycardia (rapid, but coordinated, contraction of the left ventricle out of synchrony with the rest of the heart), followed by left ventricular fibrillation (uncoordinated ventricular contractions). This causes the heart to fail to pump effectively, leading to rapid loss of consciousness and resulting in rapid onset of death. The etiology of sudden cardiac death due to emotional influences has been studied extensively in animal models by Lown, Verrier, and colleagues (see Saini & Verrier, 1989, for a review) and has been reviewed from a psychosocial perspective by Kamarck and Jennings (1991).

The above pathogenic processes and the onset of lethal outcomes are all potentiated by the secretion of epinephrine during acute stress. Circulating epinephrine can lead to clot formation, increased blood pressure resulting in stroke, or extreme increases in the demand of the heart muscle for oxygen, even at rest (Sung, Wilson, Robinson, Thadani, & Lovallo, 1988).

I strongly suspect that in many, if not most, cases of sudden death, the person has unrecognized, preexisting coronary artery disease, large increases in myocardial oxygen demand, and consequent ischemia of the heart muscle. Sudden, overwhelming emotions, especially uncontrolled fear and anger, can then act to produce a myocardial infarction, an episode of ischemia, or trigger a lethal arrhythmia in a person with preexisting disease. Nonetheless, the presence of arterial disease in cases of sudden death should not divert attention from the role of the individual's perception of the environment, interpretation of events, and emotional response as precipitating factors.

▓ Helplessness and Exposure to Uncontrollable Stress

Most episodes of loss of control do not result in death. Nevertheless, I suspect that a sense of reduced control in the face of perceived threat occurs commonly in many persons, and it is desirable to know its effects. Work on these topics has had an interesting history, and selected examples show that this work has led to a better understanding of the effects of uncontrollable stress on behavior, emotions, brain chemistry, and immune function.

To study uncontrollable stress and its effect on endocrine function, Brady and colleagues (Brady, Porter, Conrad, & Mason, 1958) tested yoked-control pairs of rhesus monkeys in a Sidman avoidance paradigm. Brady's pairs of animals received a low-level electric shock every 20 seconds unless the "executive" monkey pressed a bar, postponing the shock for 20 more seconds. The yoked monkey also had a bar and could press at will, but its behavior had no effect on the occurrence of shocks. This procedure continued for 6 hours on and 6 hours off without interruption. The executive monkeys all died with ulcers within 9-48 days on this schedule.

This study (Brady et al., 1958) attracted a great deal of attention. Ulcers were a serious disorder in the 1950s, prior to the advent of effective medication. The popular stereotype was that harried executives were the ones most likely to develop ulcers as a result of the stressful, dominant role they held, having to make important decisions and be responsible for their subordinates. The study of these executive monkeys and their yoked pairmates seemed to have a special relevance to everyday life.

Recall, however, that the yoked and executive monkeys received the same shocks. According to my model of psychological stress, the yoked (helpless) monkeys should experience greater loss of control and should therefore be under greater stress. Why did these monkeys not show ulceration and death? It turns out that there was a flaw in the execution of the study. The most active monkeys were systematically assigned to the executive role. To facilitate the experiment, Brady et al. (1958) did not randomly assign animals to their roles in the yoked pairs. They pretested all the monkeys to find those who would press the bar spontaneously and assigned these to the role of executive monkey. The executive monkeys were therefore highly active, having a spontaneous bar press rate of 15-20 responses per minute, whereas the yoked monkeys were by default less active and more placid in the face of the shocks. In following up on these interesting findings, neither Brady nor others could replicate the results.

What makes this research (Brady et al., 1958) interesting, even though the results are misleading, is that it illustrates how psychological stress can be manipulated while holding physical stress constant. Later research produced valuable information on the central nervous system mechanisms associated with severe psychological stress and ultimately led to other important findings in psychoendocrinology and psychoneuroimmunology. I will review these studies briefly.

Relevance to Ulcers in Humans

I should note that the ulcers caused in animals by uncontrollable shock are not the same kind that human ulcer sufferers have. The ulcers seen in stressed animals are interesting to stress researchers because they are manifestations of Selye's (1936) general adaptation syndrome, but they do not tell us about possible somatic or psychosomatic causes of human ulcers (see Weiner, 1991a, 1991b, for a review). We now know that most human ulcers are caused by reactivation of a chronic gastric infection by the bacterium *Helicobacter pylori*. Although it is possible that this reactivation is related to episodes of stress, this link is yet to be established.

▓ Studies of Ulceration in Rats

In pursuing the interesting leads from Brady et al.'s (1958) monkey experiments, Weiss and colleagues tested the effects of exposure to uncontrollable shock in rats. These studies are relevant to the effects of stress in humans because they suggest that the meaning of external events can alter their effect on the individual. In so doing, these studies tell us how psychological influences can modulate the physical consequences of stress.

Predictability as a Moderator of
Physical Consequences of Stress

Weiss (1970) examined whether warning animals of impending electric shock could reduce the shock's physiological effects. In understanding the stress-buffering effects of coping processes, it is useful to know if predicting the timing of an aversive event reduces its negative effects.

In Weiss (1970), predictability was manipulated in three groups of animals. One group was handled and placed in the experimental apparatus but never actually shocked, another received randomly scheduled shocks to the tail, and the third group received the same tail shocks, but each shock was preceded by a 10-second warning tone. The percentage of rats in each group that developed stress-induced ulcers differed markedly: 25% among the no-shock controls, 67% in those given a warning tone, and 100% of the unpredictably shocked rats. The unpredictably shocked animals also had the highest body temperatures, lost the most weight, and secreted the most corticosterone (the rat equivalent of cortisol). This indicates that the amygdala and central corticotropin releasing factor system, as discussed in Chapter 6, are differentially activated in the animals lacking predictability.

Because the amount of shock was identical between the two shock groups, the increased corticosterone secretion was considered to result from differences in perception of the stressful situation in the unsignalled animals. Even though the rats could not control the shocks, it was clear that the physical consequences of this stressor could be buffered by forewarning that the shock was about to occur.

Weiss (1971a) concludes that the warning signal also provided a safety signal by its absence, allowing the intervals before the tones to become safe periods. In a second study, Weiss (1971b) found that the safety of these periods could be contaminated by signaling shock with a long-lasting, gradually increasing tone that culminated in a shock. The warning tone became a conditioned stimulus, signaling impending danger throughout most of the interval between shocks and leading to high rates of ulceration. In both studies, the psychological nuances of the situation were a major determinant of the physical outcome of the stressful events.

Controllability as a Moderator of Physical Effects of Stress

Given these striking effects of predictability, Weiss (1971a) examined the ulcer-buffering effects of control over aversive events. He used a triadic design based on a traditional yoked control model. Groups of three animals were placed in individual plastic test chambers with their tails and tail-shock electrodes extending out a hole in the back. One animal, whose electrode was not connected to the shock apparatus, served as an unshocked control for the effects of handling and apparatus exposure. The other two were yoked to receive identical electric shocks. One of these was designated the executive rat, which could avoid shocks by turning a wheel, and the other was the helpless, yoked control. They underwent a Sidman avoidance paradigm in which the executive rat could avoid shocks for itself and its yoked partner by turning a wheel with its forepaws. The executive rats got far fewer ulcers than the helpless rats, apparently because they could control shocks. The results are shown in the left set of bars in Figure 7.2. Weiss (1971b) also shows that providing appropriate warning signals can further reduce the effect of the shocks on ulcer formation (the Signal condition, Figure 7.2). Therefore, both control and predictability are capable of acting as stress buffers, modulating the effect of the aversive events.

These results are opposite to the ones Brady et al. (1958) report. Instead of the overworked executives having ulcers, the helpless animals, unable to cope with the shocks, feel the greatest effect. This finding fits with the model of psychological stress described in Chapter 6. Events should have a greater negative effect on an animal when no coping behavior is available. The control afforded the executive rat buffers the effect of the stressor by providing a means of coping.

In regard to Brady et al.'s (1958) work, it is interesting to note that when Weiss (1972) reanalyzed the data for all the animals in his study, the animals that had the highest spontaneous rates of wheel turning also had the most ulcers, regardless of which condition they were in. This lends credence to the criticism of Brady's nonrandom assignment of high-responding monkeys to the executive monkey role.

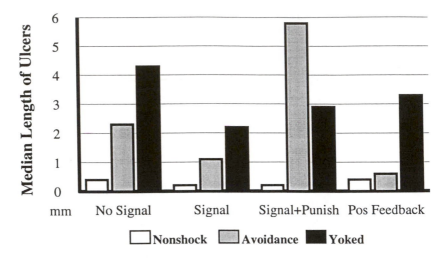

Figure 7.2. Ulcers in relation to control and quality of feedback in rats.
SOURCE: Redrawn from Weiss (1971a, 1971b).

Positive Feedback as a Moderator
of Stress Responses

In related studies, Weiss (1971b) investigated the effects of positive and negative consequences of a successful avoidance response on the amount of ulceration in the executive animals. In one condition, the executive and control rats were given a very brief shock each time the executive rat performed an avoidance response. This punishment in conjunction with a correct avoidance response resulted in the executive rats having more ulcers than the helpless rats, even though they were in control and avoiding the longer shocks that would otherwise have occurred (the Signal + Punish condition, Figure 7.2). On the other hand, when the rats were given a tone signaling that the executive rat had successfully avoided the next shock by turning the wheel, their ulcers were almost totally eliminated (the Pos Feedback condition, Figure 7.2).

The general conclusion from Weiss (1970, 1971a, 1971b) is that the psychological concomitants of the situation can enhance or reduce the effects of the stressor on the individual. The primary cause of the negative physical consequences of the shock in these studies is not the shock itself. Instead, the physical outcomes depend greatly on the psychological effect of the event. Furthermore, although these studies tell us why and how stressors can be bad for us, they also tell us how the influence of negative events can be modulated by psychological buffers—such as information about safety and successful avoidance.

Learned Helplessness and the Consequences of Lack of Control

About the time Weiss (1970, 1971a, 1971b) was carrying out these studies in his rats, Solomon, Seligman, and colleagues were exploring other aspects of uncontrollable stress in a series of studies on dogs (Seligman, Maier, & Solomon, 1971). In this work, dogs were suspended individually in hammocks to hold them in position during administration of inescapable shocks. There were three groups: a hammock-only control group, an avoidance group that could avoid the presentation of periodic shocks by pressing a plate with their noses, and a helpless yoked control group. The animals were retested 24 hours later in a shuttle box avoidance procedure.

The shuttle box consisted of two chambers separated by a low barrier. Shocks were provided to the dogs' feet by a metal grid that formed the floor of the chambers, and the shocks were signaled by a brief tone. In this training, dogs learn within a few trials to leap over the barrier to the safety of the other chamber. In fact, the control and avoidance groups from the prior training did just that. The animals that were unable to control the shocks in the sling training, however, were almost completely unable to learn this simple avoidance behavior.

Seligman and his coworkers (1971) observed marked emotional changes in the helpless dogs: These dogs exhibited greater fearfulness and anxiety. When placed in the shuttle training apparatus, they cowered in one side of the box and allowed themselves to be shocked rather than learning to jump the barrier. Seligman et al. use the term *learned helplessness* to characterize the cognitive, emotional, and performance deficits shown by the dogs after exposure to uncontrollable shock. They theorize that this apparent helplessness develops when outcomes (shocks) are not contingent on performance (attempts at escape or avoidance). The instrumental independence of outcome and behavior is presumed to result in the helpless animal learning a specific lack of dependence of outcomes on behavior, resulting in a lasting, learned deficit in the dog's ability to learn new avoidance behaviors. This learning-based formulation is bolstered by the observation that dogs bred and reared in a kennel were more susceptible to uncontrollable shock effects than captured mongrel dogs. The mongrels presumably were "immunized" by their history of successful coping with the environment outside the laboratory.

Seligman and colleagues (1971) conclude that exposure to uncontrollable shock has four major consequences:

1. The animal develops an expectation that its responses are independent of the outcomes.
2. Response initiation is reduced because responses have failed to produce consistent outcomes in the past.
3. Such animals are less able to learn to respond correctly in similar situations.
4. Depression may ensue.

In short, it appears that the animals had learned to be helpless, and that this experience led to depression. Seligman et al. therefore term this the *learned helplessness model of depression.*

Alternative Hypotheses of Behavioral Depression

Although the learning-based model of the behavioral effects of uncontrollable shock exposure was appealing, there were other viable formulations. First, Weiss's (1970, 1971a, 1971b) noted dissipation of the effect over time (approximately 48-72 hours) by his rats and Seligman et al.'s (1971) dogs argues against a learned deficit, which should have been more permanent. Second, the deficit in Weiss's rats is associated with a reduction of central nervous system norepinephrine (NE). These discrepancies led Weiss to propose a *motor activation deficit* model of uncontrollable stress. Under this model, uncontrollable stress is said to result in depletion of central nervous system NE, leading to decreased response initiation and hence motor activation deficits.

Weiss (1980) conducted a series of studies to contrast the effects of uncontrollability per se from the effects of stress. He exposed rats to a helplessness-inducing swim test in a glass cylinder half filled with water and having smooth walls. The stressfulness of the experience could be manipulated independently by altering the water temperature. This model therefore allowed the effect of stress to be evaluated independently of uncontrollability. Rats exposed to the swim test in the less-stressful room temperature water had no deficit later in a rat analogue of the shuttle box task used in dogs. In contrast, rats exposed to a highly stressful cold water swim showed the expected deficit. Clearly, in the face of equal uncontrollability, the behavioral deficit occurs only when stress levels are high.

The cold swim increased the performance-retarding effect of placing a higher barrier in the shuttle box, but it did not prevent learning to climb the barrier to avoid, again favoring the performance deficit hypothesis. Similarly, the cold swim did not interfere with learning behaviors that are very easy to perform, such as a nose poke to avoid shock. Inescapable shock functioned the same as the cold swim; it reduced shuttle box performance but did not produce a nose-poke deficit. Fourteen sessions of cold swim abolished the shuttling deficit, a result incompatible with the rats learning to be helpless. The same stress immunization occurred with 14 sessions of inescapable shock, again arguing against a learned form of helplessness.

These studies (Weiss, 1980) convincingly argue that the deficit in establishing avoidance behaviors after inescapable shock is due to a performance deficit associated with the level of the stress. With shock held constant, greater levels of stress are experienced by the helpless animals. With helplessness held constant, the performance deficit is worse with increasing stress.

Other evidence shows that the effects of the cold swim dissipated over 48 hours, enough time for the locus ceruleus to synthesize more NE. Later studies by Weiss (Weiss, Goodman, Losito, Corrigan, Charry, & Bailey, 1981) show that the performance deficit increases as central NE declines and decreases as the NE recovers. Shuttle box deficits following either uncontrollable shock or cold swim were not due to changes in other central transmitters, such as serotonin, dopamine, or acetylcholine. Weiss was able to mimic the effects of inescapable shock or cold swim by directly manipulating locus ceruleus NE. Chemical depletion of NE led to shuttle box deficits. Repeated depletion of NE did not produce shuttle box deficits. Monoamine oxidase inhibitors, drugs that reduce the breakdown of NE, counteracted the shuttle box deficit following inescapable shock.

◼ Central Neurotransmitters and Severe Stress

How would central NE become depleted by stress, and why would such a depletion alter motor activation? As noted in Chapter 6, the primary source of central NE is the noradrenergic cell bodies of the locus ceruleus of the pons. This critical nucleus communicates with the entire central nervous system. It produces a steady firing rate, thought to act as a central pacemaker, setting the background level of central nervous system activity. When alerted by signals from the amygdala (see Figure 6.3), the locus ceruleus increases its firing rate, resulting in increased alerting of the forebrain and limbic system. During transient threats, this is an adaptive means of alerting the central nervous system. Longer-term disruption of locus ceruleus firing patterns by norepinephrine depletion would chronically alter the timing of ascending activation, however. This would alter the ability of the prefrontal cortex, amygdala, and hippocampus to evaluate incoming stimuli and would disrupt the formulation and initiation of behavioral responses until the activation pattern returned to normal.

The locus ceruleus contains two sets of NE-synthesizing neurons. One set projects outward to all parts of the central nervous system (see Figure 6.4). The other set consists of small, inhibitory interneurons that internally modulate the firing of the other set. During uncontrollable shock exposure, the locus ceruleus receives high levels of input from the amygdala and hypothalamus, resulting in high firing rates. Eventually, this high level of activity depletes NE stores selectively in the smaller inhibitory interneurons. This loss of internal inhibition results in the ascending neurons, producing frequent, abnormally long bursts of activity. Because of the locus ceruleus's ability to modulate sensory processes and prefrontal-limbic communication, it is plausible that stress-induced activation of the locus ceruleus would have significant emotional and behavioral consequences. Extensive coverage of studies manipulating locus ceruleus NE are provided in Weiss et al. (1981) and Weiss (1991).

◼ Uncontrollable Shock, Norepinephrine, and Depression

Related work by Weiss (Weiss, Simson, Ambrose, Webster, & Hoffman, 1985) shows that both exposure to uncontrollable shock and chemical manipulation of NE in the locus ceruleus lead to behavioral changes corresponding to six of the eight clinical signs of human depression. These are (1) poor appetite and weight loss, (2) poor performance on tasks requiring psychomotor performance, (3) loss of energy and apparent fatigue, (4) loss of interest in usual activities (in rats this means grooming, aggressiveness, and competitiveness), (5) sleep changes, including less sleep time and more fragmented sleep, and (6) increased distractibility and indecision. The other two symptoms of human depression, thoughts of suicide and feelings of worthlessness, are not observable in rats.

One can view these studies as favoring the development of depression due to central nervous system alterations associated with uncontrollable stress. This work leaves major questions about the etiology of depression unanswered, however. Weiss's animals did not show alterations in the serotonin-containing raphe nuclei, although there is evidence that these are important in mood disturbances (Williams, 1994). In addition, the dissipation of the behavioral deficit in dogs and rats after 48-72 hours differs from the relatively long-lasting mood and behavioral changes associated with clinical depression in humans.

With such limitations in mind, these studies are significant because they show that the brainstem nuclei are responsive to psychological characteristics of the stressful situation. The outcome of this organism-environment interaction is a major determinant of subsequent behavior and moods. Most important for the present concern with psychological stress, it appears that the effect of an uncontrollable stressor on the individual depends heavily on the interpretation given to the situation and the coping options available. The effects of intermittent uncontrollable shock depend on the animal being conscious, further supporting the interpretation that these effects are due to the psychological aspects of the situation.

Control and Negative Emotions

In Chapter 6, I outlined central mechanisms of the stress response. I noted the relationship between interpretations of the world and the activity of important emotion-controlling centers of the temporal lobes. These data suggest that manipulating the interpretation of the events experienced in the course of exposure to aversive events can have powerful affective and behavioral consequences.

▓ Serotonin Mechanisms

Although Weiss's work on behavioral depression and uncontrollable aversive stress favors the view that the locus ceruleus is the critical site of altered central nervous system function, other work suggests that social stress can alter the serotonergic system associated with the brainstem raphe nuclei. Like the locus ceruleus, the raphe nuclei send fibers to many sites in the central nervous system. Descending fibers activate the motor neurons of the spinal cord, and ascending fibers travel to all parts of the cortex and to the hippocampus and amygdala. Drugs that alter serotonin levels in the brain affect mood and behavior, including feelings of depression and hostility, anger, and aggression. In recent years, treatments for mood disorders have included drugs that enhance the availability of serotonin at the synapse. There is evidence that stress may alter serotonin levels.

Uncontrollable social stress, especially early in life, may produce long-standing reductions in serotonin with consequent changes in behavior and emotions. In one group of studies (Hiley, Suomi, & Linnoila, 1992), rhesus monkeys were separated from their mothers very early in life and placed in social groups consisting entirely of similarly displaced young. These social groups were highly disrupted and did not have the normal status hierarchy that results from having members of different ages. As a result, there was a great deal of unresolved conflict and social disorganization. Young monkeys placed in peer-only groups lived there continuously prior to their introduction into normal, hierarchical social groups at 6 months of age. These peer-reared monkeys had decreased serotonin levels that persisted until at least 5 years of age. They had defective social interactions, including excessive aggression and less affiliation with others. These maternally deprived monkeys also showed exaggerated cortisol responses during social interactions. This work suggests that the stress of loss of nurturance and exposure to high levels of social disruption has a long-lasting effect on brain serotonin and behavior.

Hiley et al.'s (1992) work invites speculation that maternal nurturing acts as a buffer against the stresses of early life. Work by Meany and colleagues (Meaney et al., 1993) indicates that enhanced maternal behaviors have just such an effect. Rat pups were removed from their nests for several minutes each day during their first week of life and handled by the experimenters. When they were returned to their mothers, the pups received greatly increased levels of nurturing and attention, including licking. When tested as adults for their corticosterone responses to immobilization stress, these rats were less reactive than normally reared controls. The highly nurtured rats had elevated levels of central nervous system serotonin, exactly the opposite of the socially stressed rhesus monkeys. Further work revealed that serotonin acts to increase the synthesis of hippocampal corticosterone receptors. This increased receptor density results in enhanced negative feedback of corticosterone on the entire hypothalamic-pituitary-adrenal axis, resulting in faster dampening of stress levels of corticosterone later in life.

Research on the role of the serotonergic nuclei is more recent than that on the locus ceruleus, and there are interesting parallels in the factors influencing each of these aminergic brainstem systems and on the behavioral and emotional consequences of their disruption. Both the locus ceruleus and serotonergic nuclei appear to respond to uncontrollable stress exposure by reduced availability of their respective neurotransmitters. These changes pervasively modulate behavior, emotion, and stress proneness.

▓ Emotions and Health

The above work suggests potent, possibly long-lasting, effects of uncontrollable stress on the central mechanisms of behavior, mood, and neuroendocrine function. In addition, intermittent, uncontrollable shock suppresses immune function (Weiss & Sundar, 1992). Therefore, one may ask whether feelings of helplessness or hopelessness are related to health in a more direct way. Although evidence in humans has been difficult to obtain, recent work suggests that negative moods may be associated with poorer health outcomes.

Depression and hostility were significantly related to a variety of negative health outcomes in an extensive reanalysis of data from a large number of studies (Booth-Kewley & Friedman, 1987). In a longitudinal study, hostility predicted increased risk of coronary artery disease and mortality due to all causes (Barefoot, Dahlstrom, & Williams, 1983). More recent evidence has come from studies of immune system function. Depressed elderly persons may have a suppression of their immune systems, leaving them exposed to increased risk of infection and cancer (Solomon & Benton, 1994).

Recent epidemiological work suggests that feelings of hopelessness are related to increased risk of death due to various causes. Everson and colleagues (Everson, Goldberg, et al., 1996) studied a cohort of 2,428 men from eastern Finland and followed their health status for 6 years. At the beginning of the study, these men responded to the following statements: "I feel that it is impossible to reach the goals I should like to strive for," and "The future seems to me to be hopeless, and I can't believe that things are changing for the better," using scales of agreement ranging from 0 to 4. The cohort was divided into men scoring low (0-2), medium (3-5), and high (6-8) on the two items combined. Hopelessness scores were related in a dose-response fashion to risk of death due to all causes, including violent death and injury (Everson, Goldberg, et al., 1996). Related work shows that among men who had atherosclerosis at the start of the study, those higher in hopelessness had greater worsening of their disease over 4 years than their more optimistic counterparts (Everson, Kaplan, Goldberg, Salonen, & Salonen, in press).

■ Discussion

The material reviewed in this chapter illustrates major elements of psychological stress processes, as outlined in Chapter 6. The central feature of that model is the individual's appraisals of an event and the resources available to control it. These are critical in determining how stressful the event is. Work on aversive stress in animals shows that the psychological elements of the organism-environment interaction, such as novelty and uncontrollability, appear to enhance the stress value of the stimuli greatly and determine their physical consequences. This leads to the consideration that many of the stressors encountered in modern life, even though they pose little physical threat, may nevertheless have a significant influence on mood and health based on the person's feelings of control.

Feelings of helplessness can greatly alter the effect aversive events have on behavior, mood, and central noradrenergic and serotonergic systems. Drugs known to alter mood in humans can also alter the physical effects of the stressors in animals. The effects of these drugs parallel their effects on NE and serotonin in the brain, suggesting that the aminergic nuclei are important in the generation of emotions, along with the frontal areas and amygdala. The negative emotion states are of particular concern to the study of the effects of stress on health. They accompany behaviors that put persons at greater risk of violent death. They also predict short-term decreases in immune function and long-term negative health outcomes.

The use of yoked control designs in animal studies shows clearly that the effect of a physical stressor, such as shock, can be enhanced by lack of controllability, but it can also be buffered by behavioral control, warning of impending shock, signals indicating success in avoidance, and prior experience. As such, this work conveys both a negative and a positive message about the effects of stress on health and how they can be lessened.

I have noted in this chapter that the effect of uncontrollable stress in animals may bear a resemblance to the severe uncontrollability and overpowering emotions experienced by human victims of natural disasters. This work may, in turn, be relevant to an understanding of posttraumatic stress disorder. Although I do not deal with this syndrome in this book, I should comment that the most important effects of traumatic stress on humans are not its peripheral autonomic and endocrine effects but its effects on the central nervous system. Victims of posttraumatic stress disorder manifest exaggerated emotional responses to a wide range of stimuli and show accompanying autonomic changes. The most pervasive and disturbing aspects of the disorder are the occurrence of intrusive thoughts and dysphoric moods, including depression and anxiety, persisting for many years after the precipitating events. These changes appear to be related to long-term alterations in frontal-limbic connections and alterations in feedback to the central nervous system from the brainstem aminergic nuclei. The central nervous system mechanisms integrating the psychological stress response may undergo long-term changes due to the severe uncontrollability that accompanies traumatic stress. These central changes may appear to mediate the most troubling and persistent effects of uncontrollable stress. They may well reflect an alteration of the response bias of the system as a result of extreme levels of stress-related activation.

Turning to the basic question of this book, I asked how ideas can be translated into changes in the body. I have presented increasingly strong evidence that our ability to interpret our world and to invest that interpretation with personal meaning and emotion have a direct and powerful effect on the body. The dramatic examples of death due to devastating emotional distress provide testimony to the power of ideas to change physical well-being. The mechanisms of this translation are being increasingly well established in animal models, and these are finding confirmation in observations of humans in the laboratory and in their daily lives. The dramatic effects of a traumatic event lead us to recognize that not all persons respond alike. Different persons interpret the same event in very different ways, with equally different consequences for their well-being. In Chapter 9, I consider some of the ways that persons differ in their responses to stressful events.

SUMMARY

Psychological stress can lead to severe physical consequences, including death. The model of psychological stress presented in Chapter 6 suggests that the degree of coping and control available to an individual determines the stressfulness of an event and the physical reactions to it. In contrast, the physical effect of an aversive stressor can be entirely overcome by providing appropriate means of behavioral control and positive feedback for successful coping. Psychological stress is accompanied by negative emotions and associated behaviors, including depression, hostility, anger, and aggression. These emotions are heavily influenced by the activity of brainstem adrenergic nuclei that have extensive connections to the frontal areas of the cortex and limbic structures, including the hippocampus and amygdala. These negative emotions appear to be related to immune system function and health outcomes.

FURTHER READING

Booth-Kewley, S., & Friedman, H. (1987). Psychological predictors of heart disease: A quantitative review. *Psychological Bulletin, 101,* 343-362.

This major analysis of the relationship between negative emotions and health summarizes a great deal of literature on the subject.

Cannon, W. B. (1957). Voodoo death. *Psychosomatic Medicine, 19,* 182-190.

This engaging work on the effect of belief systems on physical well-being is highly recommended as a classic in the stress field.

Saini, V., & Verrier, R. L. (1989). The experimental study of behaviorally induced arrhythmias. In N. Schneiderman, P. Kaufmann, & S. Weiss (Eds.), *Handbook of research methods in cardiovascular behavioral medicine* (pp. 51-68). New York: Plenum.

This provides a very thorough summary of studies on sudden cardiac death due to stress in animal models.

Siegman, A. W., & Smith, T. W. (Eds.). (1994). *Anger, hostility, and the heart.* Hillsdale, NJ: Lawrence Erlbaum.

This is an extensive coverage of the relationship between hostility and the risk of coronary artery disease.

Weiss, J. M. (1980). Part V: Explaining behavioral depression following uncontrollable stressful events. *Behavioral Research and Therapy, 18,* 485-504.

This account of Weiss's early work demonstrates an important technique for studying the psychological effect of stress in animals and the role of uncontrollable stress in altering brain chemistry.

Weiss, J. M. (1991). Stress-induced depression: Critical neurochemical and electrophysiological changes. In J. Madden, IV (Ed.), *Neurobiology of learning, emotion and affect* (pp. 123-154). New York: Raven.

This is a detailed account of the alterations in locus ceruleus norepinephrine in behavioral depression and how this results in differential activation of higher centers receiving inputs from the locus ceruleus.

Williams, R. B. (1996, March). *Socioeconomic inequalities, health, and disease: An integrative theoretical review of potential neurobiological, psychosocial, biobehavioral, and cellular/molecular mediators.* Paper presented at the meeting of the Society of Behavioral Medicine, Washington, DC.

This paper provides a thoughtful integration of work on the role of stress and serotonin mechanisms in altering mood and affecting health.

The Immune System
and Behavior

Since Selye's (1936) work, we have known that high levels of cortisol occurring during states of stress can alter immune system tissues and suppress immune system responses. This led to the insight that mechanisms serving the response to a stressor have an effect on immune system function. At the same time, Selye saw infection as a stressor because it constitutes a threat to the organism and results in a set of nonspecific and specific compensatory responses. Both observations suggest that immune responses and generalized stress responses interact with each other. Since then, our recognition of the interactions between immune function and autonomic and endocrine mechanisms has grown substantially. In this chapter, I briefly describe the organization of the immune response and then provide some examples of interplay between immune function and stress-related endocrine responses. Cortical and limbic integrations ultimately modulate immune responses just as they control autonomic and endocrine responses. Other reviews of this topic are available (Kusnecov & Rabin, 1994; McEwen & Stellar, 1993; Weiss & Sundar, 1992).

Overview of the Immune System

Vertebrate organisms have evolved the capacity to detect and attack foreign cells and their own abnormal cells. Foreign organisms include bacteria, viruses, fungi, and parasites. Abnormal endogenous cells are ones altered by malignancy or infected by a virus. Immunologists refer to these collectively as *antigen,* always using the singular.

To aid in survival, the immune system recognizes antigen, neutralizes it, and then remembers specific antigen for future reference. So the immune system has the ability to perceive, respond to, and remember antigen. These are functions we usually associate with the central nervous system, and the recognition of these cognitive-like capacities in a set of nonneuronal cells residing in the body is quite striking. The immune system has been referred to as a *mobile surveillance system* (J. F. Sheridan, personal communication, August 1995) and a *circulating brain* (E. M. Sternberg, personal communication, August 1995). A thorough discussion of the immune system is provided by Kuby (1994).

The immune system comprises a set of structural components, including organs, tissues, and cells, whose activity is coordinated by a set of messenger substances. These structural components, in conjunction with immune messengers, have both innate functions and functions acquired by experience.

Structural Components of the Immune System

The structural components of the immune system are *barriers to infection,* including skin and mucous membranes, the *immune cells* that actually contact antigens and neutralize them, and the *immune organs and tissues* that produce and support the immune system cells.

The tissues of the immune system include the bone marrow, thymus, lymph nodes, and spleen. Collectively these are known as *lymphoid tissues* and are sites of production, maturation, and activation of immune system cells. The bone marrow generates the immature, undifferentiated stem cells that develop into the specialized cells that act on antigen. B cells mature in the bone marrow before entering the circulation and traveling to lymph nodes and spleen. T cells mature in the thymus, an organ located above the heart, before entering the circulation and traveling also to lymph nodes and spleen. These latter two lymphoid organs trap antigen and provide a place for activation of T and B cells by contact with the trapped antigen.

Immune System Cells

The immune system cells are all specialized, differentiated forms of white blood cells originally derived from stem cells of the bone marrow. They spend part of their time in circulation and part in the lymphatic system and spleen. There are two major classes of immune system cells: phagocytes and lymphocytes. As can be seen in Figure 8.1, these evolve through one or more stages before reaching their mature forms and becoming capable of acting as immune cells.

Phagocytes

Phagocytes consist of macrophages, neutrophils, and eosinophils. They mature from nonlymphoid stem cells and fall into two classes: monocytes and granulocytes. The name *phagocyte* implies a cell that consumes or ingests things. Specifically, phagocytes ingest and destroy antigen. Although the three types of phagocytes differ in their modes of killing, they all migrate to sites of infection, attracted by chemical messengers produced in local tissues, and ingest antigen.

Macrophages are noteworthy because they play a key role in triggering a full immune response. Macrophages break down antigen and attach the antigen particles to a specialized protein, known as the *major histocompatibility* complex (MHC). They then place the antigen-MHC complex on their surfaces and present the complex to maturing T cells. This stimulates development of T helper cells and results in production of a family of messengers called *cytokines.* The macrophages themselves are also active secreters of cytokines, which help stimulate and coordinate the immune response.

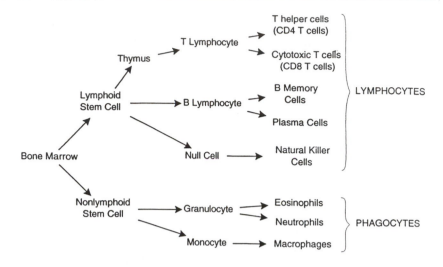

Figure 8.1. Origins of immune system cells. All immune system cells are derived from the stem cells found in bone marrow.

Lymphocytes

The lymphocytes consist of T cells, B cells, and natural killer (NK) cells. NK cells act as an innate cellular surveillance team intended to slow the development of antigen, thereby allowing time for other immune mechanisms to come into play. NK cells are genetically programmed to recognize tumor cells and virally infected cells. Using the cognitive analogy, this genetic endowment of disease-recognizing cells is a long-term memory system by which our species has learned which microorganisms are dangerous and how to destroy them.

The B lymphocytes have antigen-binding proteins called *antibodies* on their surfaces. In the surveillance process, B cells trap antigen on their surface antibodies, process the antigen, and present fragments on their surface MHC to the T cells. This B-cell-to-T-cell contact causes division and multiplication of B cells into plasma cells and memory cells. Plasma cells and B memory cells then produce antibodies specific to the antigen that originally triggered their development. Plasma cells secrete free antibodies that circulate for the duration of a disease. B memory cells live on indefinitely following contact with a novel antigen, and they continue to express specific antibodies on their surfaces. These antibodies are later found in circulation following vaccination or an episode of infectious disease.

The T lymphocytes mature in the thymus, where they become either T helper cells or cytotoxic T cells. All T cells carry antigen-recognizing molecules known as T-cell receptors.

T helper cells are the focal point of the response to invasion by exogenous antigen such as virus particles, bacteria, or fungi. Exogenous antigen is presented to T helper cells on the surface MHC of macrophages or B cells. The T helper cell has an auxiliary surface molecule, known as CD4, that assists the T cell receptor to respond to the presented antigen. In response, T helper cells secrete cytokines to activate B cells, cytotoxic T cells, macrophages, and NK cells.

The cytotoxic T cells are assisted by a different auxiliary surface receptor, known as CD8, and are specifically responsive to endogenous cells that are virally infected or tumor altered. Therefore these cells are specialized for killing the body's own cells when they have become tumor cells or have been infected by a virus.

▓ Immune System Messengers

The development, maturation, and activity of immune system cells is coordinated by a set of messengers known collectively as *cytokines* (for "cell-acting" substances). Cytokines are produced by immune system cells and in turn affect the function of distant tissues, nearby cells, and the very cells that secrete them. Table 8.1 indicates some of the principal cytokines and their actions. The most important sources of cytokines are macrophages and T helper cells. The cytokines (1) stimulate immune cell replication and division by altering gene expression; (2) stimulate immune cells to neutralize antigen and to secrete other cytokines; (3) cause B cells to form antibodies; and (4) help immune cells to recognize the antigen in the future.

Because of their signaling role, cytokines are a focal point of immune-behavior interactions. At the hypothalamus, cytokines induce illness-related behaviors, including sleep, reduced movement, and loss of appetite and sexual function. Cytokines also induce nonspecific endocrine responses via the pituitary-adrenal axis, especially secretion of stress levels of cortisol.

Having briefly considered the structure of the immune system, its cells, and the cytokines, I will consider how these act in concert during an infection.

Table 8.1   Some Principal Cytokines and Their Actions

Cytokine	Source	Actions
Interleukin 1	Macrophages B cells	Maturation and development of B cells. Activation of T helper cells, NK cells. Hypothalamic activation
Interleukin 2	T helpers	Proliferation and development of other T cells. Activation of NK cells
Interleukin 4	T helpers	Activation and proliferation of B cells. Phagocyte growth and proliferation
Interleukin 6	Macrophages T helpers	Inflammation at site of infection, plasma cell formation. Hypothalamic activation
Interleukin 10	T helpers	Macrophage activation
Interferon γ	T helpers	B cell activation, macrophage activation, NK cell activation, viral inhibition

The two functional components of the immune system include innate resistance and acquired resistance.

■ Innate Resistance

Each of us is born with innate immune capability. The body's natural resistance encompasses (1) structural defenses; (2) locally produced chemical signals that an infection is in progress; (3) innate cellular responses; and (4) nonspecific neuroendocrine-immune interactions.

Our structural defenses are positioned as a first line of defense to resist invasion of the body by pathogens. Foreign organisms that find their way into the blood or other tissues ultimately must be removed by specific mechanisms, however.

The presence of antigen produces chemical signals that attract macrophages and the other phagocytes to the site of infection, where they ingest antigen. B cells and T cells begin the innate cellular response to an infection. At birth, we have a small, innate population of reactive T cells that immediately becomes activated by our first infection and is continually modified by future antigen encounters. We are also born with a large number of genetically determined B cell antibodies. These have been shaped by selection over generations of experience with various pathogens.

The fourth component of our natural immune response includes non-specific neuroendocrine-immune system interactions. These involve cytokine-mediated secretion of epinephrine and cortisol, which acts as a global regulator of the immune response (Scheinman, Cogswell, Lofquist, & Baldwin, 1995).

Acquired Immunity and Establishment of Immune System Memory

Soon after birth, through repeated antigen exposure, our immune system matures and develops its own store of antibodies and B memory cells. A mature immune response has three phases. During the inductive phase, macrophages and T helper cells respond to antigen with specific cellular and cytokine responses. During the effector phase, mediators in lymphoid tissue take over to produce antibodies and lethal immune cells, and these activated immune cells travel to the site of an infection and destroy antigen. This results in a set of functional immune changes able to respond rapidly to later contact with the same antigen. These stages are diagrammed in Figure 8.2.

The Inductive Phase

During the inductive phase, bacteria or virus particles attract macrophages and B cells, or tumor-altered cells or virally altered cells attract macrophages and NK cells. Macrophages ingest antigen and begin secreting the cytokines interleukin-1 (IL-1) and IL-6, resulting in the effects listed in Table 8.1. Also, macrophages process the antigen for presentation on MHC to T helper cells. This causes T helper cells to stimulate themselves, by secreting IL-2, to become activated T helper cells.

T helper cell activation is the central step in the induction of the immune response because T helper cell cytokines then trigger development of specific activated T and B cell populations. The achievement of a fully developed

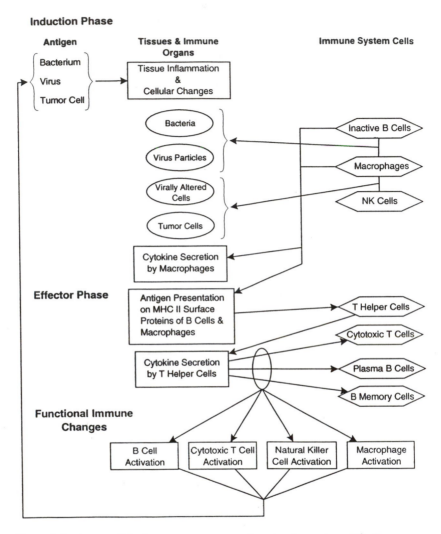

Figure 8.2. Stages of the immune response to invasion by antigen. The immune response proceeds in three stages: induction, effector phase, and functional immune changes. Each phase is associated with a different combination of immune system cells engaged in different forms of activity and functional states.

immune response can take up to 7 days, the length of time we usually take to begin to recover from a common cold.

The Effector Phase

During the effector phase of the immune response, T helper cell cytokines stimulate both major branches of the specific immune response: T cells mature into cytotoxic T cells, responsible for cell-mediated immunity; and B lymphocytes mature into plasma cells, responsible for humoral immunity. Cytokines also activate NK cells and macrophages.

In cell-mediated immunity, inactive cytotoxic T cells are stimulated by cytokines to become activated cytotoxic T lymphocytes able to destroy altered cells. In humoral immunity, B cells, performing their antigen surveillance role in the circulation or in lymph nodes, come in contact with antigen and present it to T helper cells already activated by IL-2. This causes the activated T helper cells to secrete IL-2, IL-4, IL-6, and interferon-γ. The B cells then differentiate and multiply to become either B memory cells or plasma cells. The plasma cells travel to lymph nodes, the spleen, and the sites of active infection and begin producing large quantities of free antibodies that enter circulation. These circulating free antibody particles can surround and inactivate antigen. The steps are summarized in the middle portion of Figure 8.2.

To summarize the effector phase, antigen presentation to T helper cells and their resultant IL-2 secretion results in production of cell-killing cytotoxic T lymphocytes, antibody production by plasma cells, and B memory cells. These resultant cells are shown in the lower right portion of Figure 8.2.

Functional Immune Changes

The inductive phase also results in the production of long-lived T memory cells and the B memory cells that carry specific antibodies. At this stage, the full immune response cycle has been completed and the system is primed to ward off future attacks by the same antigen.

■ The Behavior-Immune Interface

Selye's (1936) work suggests an interaction between immune function and stress responses. In fact, there are four points of contact:

1. The immune system signals the central nervous system with cytokines.

2. The central nervous system regulates the immune response through the pituitary-adrenocortical axis.

3. Immune system cells have receptors for epinephrine.

4. The organs of the immune system are innervated by both branches of the autonomic nervous system (Felten & Felten, 1991).

This two-way communication opens many possibilities for considering the behavioral interactions with the immune system.

Immune-to-Behavior Communication

In discussing cytokines, I noted that some of these are able to reach the hypothalamus, where they induce secretion of stress levels of cortisol and produce what immunologists call *illness behaviors.*

In animal studies, injection of IL-1 or IL-6 either systematically or into the third ventricle, adjacent to the hypothalamus, leads to a full range of illness behaviors. The hypothalamus has numerous cytokine receptors, suggesting a specific signaling role to this important regulatory area.

We are all familiar with the powerful feeling of being sick. This malaise has general characteristics regardless of the specific illness we may have. At the beginning, we may notice nothing more than a vague mood disturbance, a feeling of impatience and irritability. Soon we begin to feel that all is not well, gradually recognizing that we are actually sick. Shortly after, we find ourselves wanting to withdraw from activities, to become inactive, and to sleep if possible. At the same time, we lose our appetite for food and our interest in pleasurable activities such as listening to music, seeing a movie, or engaging in sex.

The generation of illness behaviors is paralleled by activation of stress levels of corticotropin releasing factor (CRF) via the magnocellular portion of the paraventricular nucleus of the hypothalamus. This activation of the stress-related part of the CRF system results in the secretion of high levels of cortisol, involving alterations in mood and other central nervous system changes.

Behavior-to-Immune Communication

The recognition that components of stress responses can alter the immune system provides an important key for thinking about one way that immune function can be altered by behavior. I have discussed in previous chapters how emotions and cognitions can alter activity in important limbic structures, including the hippocampus and amygdala. These in turn can signal the hypothalamus to modify both hormonal secretions via the adrenal gland and sympathetic outflow by the autonomic nervous system.

The adrenal and sympathetic components of the stress response have pervasive influences on the immune system. Lymphoid tissues, including thymus, spleen, and lymph nodes, receive both sympathetic and parasympathetic neurons (Felten & Felten, 1991). Changes in autonomic activity will affect these tissues and alter the development and activity of populations of lymphocytes, including NK, T, and B cells. So the cell populations needed to orchestrate the destruction of invading organisms are directly altered by autonomic activity accompanying emotional activation and stress.

Lymphocytes have β adrenoreceptors and cortisol receptors. The effects of catecholamines on lymphocyte receptors can be complex, both increasing and decreasing indicators of immune system function. For example, epinephrine stimulation of β receptors can reduce the ability of NK cells to enter lymph nodes, where they usually contact and neutralize antigen (Ottaway & Husband, 1992). At the same time, epinephrine can cause splenic contraction, releasing stored lymphocytes into the general circulation and increasing their ability to travel to sites of infection. β adrenergic activation accompanying acute stress can increase NK cell numbers in circulation but also decrease the ability of T cells to multiply to appropriate stimuli (Bachen et al., 1995). This range of effects is a caution against thinking that stress always impairs the immune system. Instead, it is important to consider the specific situations under which enhancements and decreases in function may occur.

The immune system also has important interactions with the hypothalamic-pituitary-adrenocortical axis (HPAC). Stress levels of cortisol can inhibit immune function in several ways, including the following:

1. decreased macrophage expression of MHC in response to IL-2 or interferon-γ;
2. decreased macrophage cell ingestion;
3. decreased IL-1 production by macrophages;
4. decreased IL-2 production by T cells;
5. decreased production of CD4 cells;
6. suppressed activity of B lymphocytes; and
7. decreased activity of NK cells.

These changes amount to a reduction of the frequency and strength of immune system messages and a reduction of the numbers and activity of cells carrying out immune responses. In contrast to the effects of sympathetic activity and circulating epinephrine, cortisol may exert largely deleterious effects on immune function. This may call attention to situations and emotional states accompanied by cortisol elevations as being particularly worthy of study as potential impairments to immune function.

These thoughts lead one to consider the interface between immune function and our emotions and behaviors. This interface consists of integrated neural and hormonal messages that allow for communication in both directions. There are several examples of this communication at work, and these all invite interesting speculations about the relationship between health and behavior. Immunologists formerly viewed the immune system as highly autonomous in its actions, responding only to the presence of antigen. More recent views stress a hierarchy of controls involving the hypothalamus, limbic system, and cerebral cortex. Felten and colleagues have suggested that the immune system is ultimately under behavioral control (Felten et al., 1991).

Behavior-Immune Interactions and Health Indicators

The interaction of immune system function and stress mechanisms can be illustrated by several examples. The first example concerns stress effects on immune system activation to viral challenge and on reactivation of latent viruses. The second has to do with altered risk for arthritis due to deficient cortisol secretion. The third example concerns changes in specific immune system indicators during life stressors.

Stress, Immune Response to Viral Challenge, and Viral Reactivation

I have noted that stress can reduce immune system function. Under normal circumstances, infection with an active influenza strain or vaccination with an inactive virus will produce an immune response measurable in the number of antibody particles found in the circulation. Increases in stress levels and their associated elevations in cortisol and sympathetic nervous system activity can suppress the immune system activation that usually follows these viral challenges, however. For example, repeated restraint stress in mice can alter production of antibodies and lower T cell activation in response to infection with the influenza virus (Sheridan & Dobbs, 1994). Similarly, hepatitis B vaccine produces a stronger antibody response in medical students who report better social support and less global stress (Glaser, Kiecolt-Glaser, Bonneau, Malarkey, & Hughes, 1992). These studies suggest that stress and negative emotional states are likely to lower the immune system's ability to mount a successful response to challenge with an active virus or a vaccination. The specific mechanisms of such a behavior-immune interaction remain to be fully identified, although elevated cortisol may be a mediator.

Suppressed immune function can also be seen in the reactivation of latent viruses, such as herpes simplex and Epstein-Barr, during times of stress (see Bonneau, 1994, for a review). After an initial infection, these viruses become dormant in cell bodies of the sensory and autonomic neurons innervating the originally infected tissues. They can remain dormant for long periods. Emotional distress appears to trigger reactivation of these latent viruses, as seen in the recurrent outbreak of fever blisters in persons undergoing life stress (Jemmott & Locke, 1984) and in adolescents who tend to develop mononucleosis when overworked and underrested. Medical students undergoing the stress of examinations are more likely to have outbreaks of herpes if they are lacking in social support (Glaser, Kiecolt-Glaser, Speicher, & Holliday, 1985). Similarly, exam stress is associated with high levels of antibody to Epstein-Barr virus, suggesting reactivation of latent infections (Glaser et al., 1987). Similar indicators of decreased immune surveillance are seen in men undergoing divorce and experiencing poor marital relationships (see Keller, Shiflett, Schliefer, & Bartlett, 1994).

The mechanisms of viral reactivation are not fully understood, although both sympathetic nervous system activity and hypothalamic-pituitary-adrenal activation may be involved. Jenkins and Baum (1995) note that reactivation of herpes simplex virus is preceded by high levels of nerve growth factor. Nerve growth factor is produced in surrounding tissues in response to sympathetic nerve activity. It is possible that sympathetic activation, associated with acute stress and negative emotional states, may lead to increases in nerve growth factor, triggering reactivation of latent herpes viruses in affected nerves and target tissues. Viral latency is also maintained by active immune surveillance, and suppression of immune function may permit reactivation to occur. The magnitude of cortisol response to acute stressors in the laboratory appears to be significantly correlated in young men with levels of antibodies to Epstein-Barr virus, suggesting greater reactivation of the virus in the most stress-reactive persons (Cacioppo, in press). Therefore, cortisol levels high enough to suppress immune function may also permit reactivation of herpes viruses.

Increased Rheumatoid Arthritis Susceptibility and Altered HPAC Function

Illness is itself a stressor and peripheral cytokines find their way to the hypothalamus, where they cause the secretion of stress levels of cortisol. What is the adaptive value of the immune system generating stress levels of cortisol capable of impairing the immune response? The answer seems to be that the immune response works best when it is regulated. On the one hand, if the immune system is underresponsive, we risk being overwhelmed by invading organisms. On the other hand, in the absence of regulation, the immune response would run unchecked, with massive quantities of inflammatory cytokines being secreted. Too much inflammation can damage healthy tissue, causing problems above and beyond the effects of the illness itself. One reason we take aspirin when we are sick is to reduce inflammatory responses. For the same reason, we put ice on an injury. The healing is faster and more problem free if the injured tissue does not become too inflamed. High levels of cytokines can be deadly. In the case of toxic shock syndrome, the victim can die within hours from an unregulated immune response.

During the early phases of an infection, the HPAC produces cortisol in response to cytokines from peripheral infection. Similarly, the hypothalamic-adrenomedullary axis is stimulated to produce epinephrine. The high levels of cortisol production induced by the activation of the HPAC suppress inflammation at the site of infection and control cellular responses by lymphoid tissues. This results in lowered production of immune cells, fewer cytokines, and less inflammation of infected tissues, further reducing cytokine production. This negative feedback relationship between the cytokine signaling system and the HPAC during infection is essential to the proper regulation of the immune response.

The dangers of an unregulated immune system are illustrated by research on the cause of the inflammatory disease rheumatoid arthritis. In this form of arthritis, the joints become chronically inflamed and are swollen and deformed. The disease is crippling, often making it impossible for the victim to work. Women are about four times as likely to develop rheumatoid arthritis as men. Women also have more active immune systems than men do (Morell, 1995). Research into the causes of this debilitating and painful disease has concentrated on two companion strains of inbred rats known as the Lewis and Fisher strains. The story of this odd couple of the rodent world is important because it illustrates how behavioral mechanisms related to the stress response, acting through the HPAC, can affect mechanisms of disease.

The Lewis rat is highly susceptible to arthritis. Researchers have long known that infecting Lewis rats with streptococcus bacterium ultimately resulted in arthritis of the paw joints. It seems that in these rats, the strep infection ran unchecked and resulted in the development of severe, chronic joint inflammation. This produced joint swelling and deformity, as seen in human arthritis sufferers. On the other hand, a close relative of the Lewis rat, the Fisher rat, is highly resistant to arthritis. Attempts to induce persistent inflammation by infecting these rats with various bacterial strains failed to produce any untoward effects. Eventually, it was discovered that the differing fates of these two rat strains were determined by differences in their HPAC reactivity.

Sternberg and her colleagues at the National Institute of Mental Health (Sternberg et al., 1989) discovered that the Lewis rat is highly deficient in its ability to secrete corticosterone during stress or in response to normal metabolic stimuli. On the other hand, the Fisher rat was found to be a corticosterone hypersecretor—anything likely to cause a rat to secrete corticosterone produces an exaggerated response by these rats. The difference between these rat strains in HPAC reactivity and disease susceptibility is more than coincidence; the difference in corticosterone secretion was found to underlie the difference in disease proneness.

These rat strains are histocompatible; the genes encoding their MHCs are identical, and they can accept tissue donations from each other without danger of rejection. Through a careful series of tissue transplantation experiments, these scientists (Sternberg et al., 1989) determined that the two strains differ in their hypothalamic areas controlling synthesis and secretion of CRF. By transplanting portions of the hypothalamus from the Fisher to the Lewis rat, it is possible to make the Lewis recipient normally resistant to arthritis. Similarly, removing these portions of the hypothalamus from the Fishers made them as vulnerable to arthritis as the Lewis rats. Apparently these hypothalamic transplants augmented the deficient stress corticosterone secretion in the Lewis rat.

The relationship between deficient HPAC responsiveness and rheumatoid arthritis leads to the speculation that emotions acting through this axis can alter arthritis susceptibility. Sternberg (Sternberg, Wilder, Chrousos, & Gold, 1991) proposes that deficient HPAC activity accompanying depression may link depression with enhanced susceptibility to, or greater severity of, rheumatoid arthritis.

Altered Immune Function and Life Stress in Humans

Studies of artificial stressors in the laboratory have many advantages, but they do not readily allow us to study how people are affected by events in their daily lives. Studies of life stressors and their effects on health and health indicators can give us useful insights into the effects of stress on health.

One method of studying life stress is to follow persons exposed to natural disasters for their psychological reactions and physical consequences. Such events can result in prolonged feelings of helplessness and psychological distress associated with altered endocrine function and immune system indicators. Baum (1990) examined residents of the area around the Three-Mile Island nuclear plant in Pennsylvania following the radiation leak and reactor shutdown. After the accident, compared to controls, residents felt more psychological distress, had higher urinary catecholamines, and showed lowered levels of T, B, and NK cells, and they had higher antibodies to herpes simplex virus. Residents also had a prolongation of cardiovascular responses to mental arithmetic stress. Years after the accident, some residents had higher blood pressures than before it occurred. These changes indicate a state of chronic stress with depressed immune function and elevated sympathetic nervous system activity.

Other studies of stress in daily life concern the effects of examinations on students and daily stressors in a community sample. Medical students predictably show higher levels of psychological distress and elevated blood pressure on days of major exams (Sausen, Lovallo, Pincomb, & Wilson, 1992). Students report more illness surrounding exam periods and have higher antibodies to Epstein-Barr virus and lower T cell activation and cytokine secretion (Glaser et al., 1987). In a community sample, reported daily life stress was associated with lowered activation of the immune response to challenge with a novel, harmless antigen (Stone et al., 1994).

Deficiencies of immune function may exist in relation to the experience of stress in the school setting and possibly the workplace.

Although studies such as the above focus on immune system indicators, others have examined actual susceptibility to illness in persons experiencing stressful life events. Kawachi and colleagues (1995) have shown that nurses who perform rotating shift work for more than six years of their working lives have a significantly increased risk of heart disease and heart attack than nurses who work normal daytime shifts. Although heart disease is not usually associated with immune system dysregulation, recent models of the athero-genic process give a major role to cytokine production in the affected arteries and to macrophages and other phagocytes in their role as scavengers of damaged cells and lipids in the atherosclerotic lesion (Hajjar & Nicholson, 1995). This study (Kawachi et al., 1995) provides significant evidence of the deleterious effects of prolonged stress on health.

Similar evidence comes from a study of the effects of acute infection with cold viruses. Cohen (1994) and coworkers exposed volunteers to nose drops containing one of several varieties of cold viruses or to a saline solution and followed them for several days to note which ones developed actual colds, had subclinical signs of respiratory changes, or had immune system responses indicating an infection. Volunteers experiencing more negative life events along with poor coping responses and negative emotional states were more likely to have higher rates of infection and to contract colds. Negative life events were the strongest predictor of these reactions.

The final example of the effects of emotional stress on immune function comes from the effects of difficult personal relationships. Kiecolt-Glaser and colleagues have conducted a longitudinal study of the psychological and health effects on elderly persons involved in chronic care of a spouse with Alzheimer's disease. Alzheimer's is an untreatable, progressive dementia that severely alters the personality and impairs communication and cognitive capacity. It places a severe burden on spouses who are caregivers. The disease signals a permanent and irreversible change in a loved one and a loss of support within the marriage. Bearing the burden of such a demand constitutes a meaningful, long-term life stressor to the elderly caregiver.

The act of caring for an Alzheimer's patient is demanding, and caregivers usually have few social contacts and little time to spend with the ones they do have. They experience physical and mental fatigue and negative emotions, especially depression. In one study (Kiecolt-Glaser, Malarkey, Cacioppo, & Glaser, 1994), the spouses who were most distressed by their partner's dementia and lowest in social support also showed lowered levels of cellular immunity and had more frequent respiratory tract infections. In the laboratory, the caregivers who had the largest heart rate increases to mental arithmetic also had the largest cortisol responses and the greatest alterations in NK cell function to the stressor. Compared to age-matched controls, caregivers of Alzheimer's patients also show slower healing of superficial wounds to the skin, a process dependent on cytokine production and macrophage response (Kiecolt-Glaser, Marucha, Malarkey, Mercado, & Glaser, 1995). Other work supports a linkage between the chronic stress of caregiving, cardiovascular responses to mental stress, cortisol activation, and immune system modulation (Uchino, Cacioppo, Malarkey, & Glaser, 1995). These findings suggest a relationship between immune function and life stress accompanied by adrenocortical and cardiovascular activation, although the specific linkages remain to be studied.

▓ Stress Buffers, Positive Emotions, and Physical Health

The examples of behavior-immune interactions above concern the effect of negative emotions and life stress on the immune system. Whether parallel enhancements of immune function accompany positive behavioral states is not presently known. The possible buffering effects of positive emotions, positive human relationships, and enhanced feelings of self-efficacy are thought to ameliorate the negative effects of life stress on immune function, however (see Kiecolt-Glaser & Glaser, 1992, for a review). Although there is little research on enhanced immune function in relation to positive emotions, some suggestive examples from the psychological literature encourage one to think that behavior can be used in positive ways to counteract the effects of life stresses and disease. For example, Berk and colleagues (1989) demonstrate that several minutes of laughter in subjects viewing a humorous film led to lowered epinephrine and cortisol levels, suggesting that immune cells and organs may also have been affected. Another study (Keller et al., 1994) indicates that the effects of emotional expression can ameliorate the effects of trauma, leading to improved psychological status and immune function. Students were asked to write about traumatic events in their lives or about emotionally neutral events every day for 4 days. Six months later, those who expressed themselves about their traumas were happier and less depressed. They also had better lymphocyte activity, suggesting improved immune function relative to controls.

Spiegel (Spiegel, Bloom, Kraemer, & Gottheil, 1989) investigated the effects of 1 year of weekly group psychotherapy on the survival of women who had developed recurrence of breast cancer. Women who participated in these groups survived significantly longer compared to those who were given medical care only. The women in the treatment groups formed strong personal bonds and learned to express freely their emotions, even negative ones, to the supportive members of their groups. Furthermore, most of the group members spontaneously chose to continue their association after the formal period of their group therapy. This suggests a positive effect of the strong emotional bonding and social support that developed among these women. Although this study indicates an association among positive social relationships, emotional status, and health, we are not yet aware of the mechanisms that may have mediated this relationship. The study of how positive human experiences may enhance health will undoubtedly be an active area for many years to come.

▨ Discussion

The immune system is affected by the stress response and activation of the immune system to fight an infection is in itself a form of stress response. This interplay between immune system and stress-related mechanisms is mirrored by a set of immune-behavioral interactions. On the surface, it is remarkable that such interactions should occur at all. Most of us, including most psychologists and biologists, had long held an implicit, strongly dualistic notion of biology and behavior.

On the one hand, immunologists were concerned with hormonal and cellular mechanisms that protect us from invading organisms. These mechanisms were seen to be highly autonomous, operating without our awareness or conscious control. On the other hand, psychologists were interested in the conscious and not-so-conscious ways we direct our overt and covert behaviors to operate in the world. The emotions and conscious experiences that accompany and serve these behaviors are a large part of what we call our psychology. And, in a sort of crude computer analogy, we thought of our bodies as the hardware and our psychology as the software running through, and even controlling, the hardware, but not changing the hardware. In other words neither the behavioral community nor the biological community was prepared for the full implications of the emerging view that our immune system and our behavior are not just separate entities sharing the same space. They are in fact different expressions of the same biobehavioral process.

If we say that our immune system and our behavior are really only different ways of seeing the same survival process, we begin to recognize that behavior affects our health in a basic way, by modulating the very system that fights invading organisms. Just as important, we recognize that our state of health and immune function affects our emotions and behavior. The details of this interplay are becoming increasingly well understood, contributing to a growing reformulation of dualistic ideas about biology and behavior.

The previous examples of immune response to viral challenge are particularly useful for illustrating the relationship between stress and changes in immune function. These studies allow clear interpretations about the changed immune status of the individual as a function of stress. Studies of single organ or cell function are less clearly interpretable in terms of global health consequences of immune status.

Also, many lab-based studies use stressors that are at best moderately stressful and emotionally neutral or mildly aversive (e.g., demanding work on a mental arithmetic task). The ability to extrapolate to real-life disasters and severely aversive situations is limited.

At present, we have an increasingly appealing case that emotions and cognitions can alter the function of the immune system. Whether these can in fact alter short-term or long-term health is less certain. The mechanisms by which these connections may come about remain to be explored.

SUMMARY

The immune system is a highly evolved collection of structural defense mechanisms, specialized cells, and chemical messengers. Together, these allow us to survive in a hostile environment containing viruses, bacteria, and other harmful foreign material. The immune system operates in two-way communication with the brain and the endocrine system. Because of this extensive communication, the immune system can influence how we feel and behave. Similarly, our behavior affects the operation of the immune system. Negative emotional states involving feelings of distress are associated with endocrine and autonomic changes that can inhibit immune system function. This results in decreased resistance to new infections and reactivation of latent infections. Studies of humans exposed to brief and prolonged stressors illustrate an array of specific immune alterations and lower resistance to disease. A few encouraging studies suggest that positive emotional experiences and strong social support networks can enhance immune system function and perhaps improve health.

FURTHER READING

Ader, R., Felten, D., & Cohen, N. (1990). Interaction between the brain and the immune system. *Annual Review of Pharmacology and Toxicology, 30,* 561-602.

This is a brief review of neural-immune interactions.

Ader, R., Felten, D., & Cohen, N. (Eds.). (1991). *Psychoneuroimmunology* (2nd ed.). San Diego: Academic.

This volume provides an updated edition of the classic volume on psychoneuroimmunology, an advanced work dealing with a wide range of general themes and specialized topics.

Glaser, R., & Kiecolt-Glaser, J. K. (Eds.). (1994). *Handbook of human stress and immunity.* San Diego: Academic.

This thorough coverage of topics in stress and immune system function includes a heavy emphasis on human work in behavioral medicine.

Kuby, J. (1994). *Immunology* (2nd ed.). New York: Freeman.

This is a well-illustrated and thorough textbook on immunology.

Vitkovic, L., & Koslow, S. H. (Eds.). (1994). *Neuroimmunology & mental health* (DHHS Publication No. NIH 94-3774). Washington, DC: Government Printing Office.

This is a concise review of current trends in immunology research in behavioral medicine.

Individual Differences in Central, Autonomic, and Endocrine Responses to Stress

In earlier chapters, I discussed the central nervous system origins of stress responses and their autonomic and endocrine consequences. It is important to recognize that not all persons respond to stressors in the same way. When faced with potential threats, persons differ in their primary and secondary appraisals and in their physiological responses. Such differences among persons have implications for how we think about stress mechanisms and health.

As a means of organizing this discussion of individual differences, I will make use of the model of stress mechanisms outlined in Chapter 6. I will describe two major ways people may differ in response to psychological stressors. Persons may differ because of their cognitive and emotional characteristics, reflected in how they interpret and experience events, or because of their hypothalamic and brainstem activation, reflected in cardiovascular and endocrine responses. Finally, I will consider implications of these differences for health and disease.

▨ Individual Differences in Stress Responses May Be Determined by Reactions at Several Levels in the Central Nervous System

There are potentially four levels at which persons may differ in how they react to threats. These four levels correspond to major components of the model of central nervous system components of the psychological stress response in Figure 6.3. First, persons may differ in their primary and secondary appraisals of events and available coping resources. These processes correspond to activities of the prefrontal areas, the insular cortex, the hippocampus, and the amygdala. Evaluations and emotions originating at these higher levels in the central nervous system then alter the strength and direction of responses generated by the hypothalamus and brainstem. Second, as one moves down the system, hypothalamic areas such as the Hypothalamic Area Controlling Emotional Responses (HACER) may be more or less reactive to a given set of messages from the amygdala. That is, inborn factors or experience may alter the initial responsiveness of the hypothalamus to descending activation, and this may constitute a consistent source of differences among persons in how they respond to stress. Third, in the same way, hypothalamic areas responsible for outputs to lower centers, such as the paraventricular nucleus, may react to a greater or lesser degree to a set of messages from the HACER. Finally, brainstem centers may be more or less reactive in two ways: (1) the aminergic nuclei, such as the locus ceruleus, may differ in the strength of the signals they send to the rest of the central nervous system, and (2) the outputs to the peripheral organs via the intermediolateral cell column, the nucleus of the solitary tract, and the pituitary may differ from person to person.

▨ Persons May Differ in Stress Reactivity Because of Inborn Factors or Experience

As noted in Chapter 7, experience may have a lasting effect on responses to stressors. Animals undergoing severe threat from the environment with limited coping options develop lasting alterations in behavior, emotions, and physiological function. Similarly, the work I cited in Chapter 7 on the effects of unstable social hierarchies on young monkeys indicates that relatively permanent changes in levels of central nervous system serotonin can result from early maternal deprivation and exposure to social conflict.

In addition to the role of experience, genetic factors can determine differences in psychological and physiological responses to stress. The clearest evidence of inborn differences in stress response comes from studies of the spontaneously hypertensive rat, an animal that is hyperreactive both behaviorally and physiologically (Knardahl & Hendley, 1990). Similarly, monkeys raised in identical circumstances and from the same species show large individual differences in heart rate responses to behavioral threats as well as differing in aggressiveness and affiliative tendencies (Kaplan, Manuck, Clarkson, & Prichard, 1985).

▓ Sources of Individual Difference in Stress Responses

Four levels in the central nervous system can determine differences among persons in stress reactivity.

Individual Differences in Evaluative and Emotional Processes

The first item concerns evaluative and emotional responses to events, processes associated with primary and secondary appraisals. Two converging lines of evidence suggest that stable differences may exist among persons in the formation of situational judgments and the development of the emotions that accompany them. The first line of evidence concerns neurophysiological differences in prefrontal and limbic functions based on brain imaging and electroencephalographic (EEG) techniques. The second line comes from traditional work on personality differences and accompanying physiological differences to appropriate challenges.

Neurophysiological Evidence on Prefrontal-Limbic Connections and Emotions

People differ in how they interpret events and how they form emotions in relation to these interpretations. Interpretation of events and their evaluation based on experience occurs in working memory. Recent work by Goldman-Rakic (see Ungerleider, 1995) shows that areas of the prefrontal cortex are differentially activated during tasks requiring working memory. These cortical areas are also tied to the architecture of sensory systems and are accessible to long-term memory. This allows the prefrontal cortex to have the benefit of prior experience while processing current inputs along with emotional reactions associated with general contextual cues. One may therefore think of working memory as a way for bringing together the highest integration of our past and present experience with the benefit of our emotional evaluations of these. The influence of prior experience on working memory suggests that stable, but not completely fixed, differences among persons may be formed by life experiences, and these experiences may alter the evaluation of current events. These evaluations are intimately tied to activity of limbic structures. LeDoux (1993) considers the hippocampus to be critical for the recall of events in our lives and the amygdala to be critical for recall of the contextual aspects of these events.

Given that we plausibly form primary and secondary appraisals in working memory, and that this process depends on activity in prefrontal regions, one could ask how appraisals and their associated emotions come to differ among persons. Our understanding of individual differences in emotional disposition comes from two sources. The first source is the increasing awareness that positive and negative emotions are served by different subsystems in the frontal and temporal lobes. The second source of information indicates that the frontal lobes may be asymmetric for the generation of emotions and that persons may differ in the degree to which they characteristically activate structures on one side or the other.

Gray (1987, 1991) proposes two distinct frontal-limbic systems responsible for interpretation of incoming events and formulation of responses. One is the *behavioral inhibition system,* thought to play a central role in anxiety. This system seems to organize autonomic and behavioral responses to aversive conditioned stimuli. In animals, the freezing response seems to be a complete behavioral complex encompassing immobility, heightened attention, and motor preparedness in the face of threat. It has been viewed as a behavioral pattern that develops in preparation for the active component of the fight-flight response. Gray's system incorporates the septohippocampal system with fibers ascending from brainstem nuclei, such as the locus ceruleus, that themselves receive inputs from the amygdala. The septal area of the limbic system, often referred to as the *pleasure center* of the brain, has connections to and from the amygdala and hippocampus. It may therefore assist in tagging material in working memory with a positive or negative emotional valence.

Gray (1987, 1991) also postulates a *behavioral approach* system that responds to appetitive stimulation and is linked to positive emotions and motivates exploration and appetitive behavior. Based on such evidence, Cacioppo and Berntson (1994) suggest that Gray's approach and withdrawal systems are differentially distributed in the left and right hemispheres, respectively. These authors argue that negative emotions associated with stressful events are differentially activated by right hemisphere structures. Given that prior experience will affect both memories and conditioned responses to situations, the behavioral approach and inhibition systems can motivate both behaviors and physiological responses in conjunction with primary and secondary appraisals.

In agreement with this postulated emotion-relevant asymmetry, Davidson and colleagues (Tomarken, Davidson, Wheeler, & Doss, 1992) have observed individual differences in the asymmetry of EEG activity measured over the left and right frontal areas. Persons with greater activation of left frontal regions tend to react positively to many situations and to be highly resistant to depression. Conversely, persons with greater right-sided activation are prone to negative mood states and depressive episodes. Work by others has shown that depressed individuals have reduced metabolic activity in the left prefrontal cortex. As indicated in Figure 6.3, prefrontal areas modulate activity in the hippocampus and amygdala of the temporal lobes by way of the insular cortex and septohippocampal system. I noted that patients with prefrontal damage may show inappropriate and poorly controlled emotional outbursts, as if the limbic centers responsible for releasing basic emotional expression were not being controlled appropriately by their related prefrontal areas. Davidson's work on the roles of the left and right prefrontal cortexes indicates that asymmetric frontal activation results in asymmetric modulation of the limbic areas responsible for emotion.

This modulation asymmetry appears to be an important determinant of individual differences in emotional experience, and it appears to be a relatively stable, trait-like characteristic. For example, shy, inhibited children are low in left frontal alpha EEG activation, and shyness is one of the most stable emotional-behavioral traits. Adults show long-term consistency in resting alpha asymmetry and in their accompanying emotional dispositions. Right and left frontal EEG activity varies as a function of exposure to negative and positive events, respectively, and in relation to the negative and positive emotions accompanying those events. Diazepam, a potent antianxiety drug that acts on brainstem aminergic nuclei, increases approach behavior and increases left frontal activation in rhesus monkeys.

This research provides a neurophysiologically based view of the differences among persons in their evaluative processes and related emotions. This view helps us appreciate that there are persistent neurophysiological differences among persons underlying their characteristic outlooks and moods. These differences are almost surely a combination of inborn tendencies and life experiences. I noted, in Chapter 7, research by Meaney (Meaney et al., 1993) showing that rats developed long-term elevations in serotonergic function based on repeated handling of stress early in life and the resultant added mothering. In contrast, serotonin deficiencies were related to negative moods, aggression, and lack of social affiliation.

Personality Dispositions, Emotions, and Responses to Stress

If persons differ neurophysiologically in ways that affect personality dispositions and evaluative tendencies, the model of psychological stress in Chapter 6 would lead us to expect parallel differences in how people engage their hypothalamic and brainstem areas controlling peripheral activation. Persons who have strong emotion traits tend to act these out in their overt behavior and, I suspect, in their physiological responses. I will discuss some examples drawn from traditional personality based formulations comparing persons varying in levels of trait hostility.

Suarez (Suarez & Williams, 1989) has shown that persons high in cynical hostility, as measured by self-reports on the Cook-Medley Ho scale, produce larger blood pressure responses to a task performed immediately after a social encounter with a rude laboratory assistant. Observations from a related study by Everson (Everson, McKey, & Lovallo, 1995) illustrate how social cues can trigger specific evaluations in hostility-prone persons and how these can alter physiological responses. Everson interviewed young men to assess their potential for hostility. The most- and least-hostile men were invited back to the laboratory for a second experiment, ostensibly to measure how blood pressure was affected by mental challenges. Each person worked on two identically difficult mental arithmetic tasks separated by a 20-minute rest. One third of the subjects served as controls and worked on both tasks under neutral conditions. The others were harassed during the rest period between the tasks.

At the end of the rest interval, a new, female experimenter entered the testing room and rudely announced that the original experimenter had forgotten a prior appointment and that she would now have to finish the testing, conveying a sense of irritation at this inconvenience. She removed the subject's reading material just as a phone outside the door rang. She then held a staged conversation, gossiping about friends' hairdos and dating habits, at last remarking in a bored voice that she had to "finish up with this guy in here." She then made several gratuitous harassing comments during the second task.

The subjects' reports provide insight into differences in how the high- and low-hostile men saw the interpersonal dynamics of the social situation. One high-hostile subject became extremely irate and announced that he would not participate in a study conducted by such rude and uncaring people! (Naturally, he was debriefed and told about the purpose of the study, as were all other subjects.) High-hostile men more often felt that the experimenter was directing her callous attitude toward them in a personal way, whereas low-hostile men often imagined that the new experimenter was merely having a bad day. These reports indicate an important difference in the groups' primary appraisals of the situation. When questioned about their suspicions, about twice as many low-hostile as high-hostile men had doubts about the scenario. It was as if the high-hostile men were prepared to react from a hostile standpoint, and when the social stimuli were presented, they reacted without reflection. Structured mood reports were taken during the study. High-hostile men reported feeling more global activation and a greater sense of distress than low-hostile men.

Along with these appraisal differences, the high- and low-hostile men also responded to the second task with different levels of cardiovascular activation. Figure 9.1 shows the response differences from the first to the second tasks for harassment and the control condition. The high-hostile men

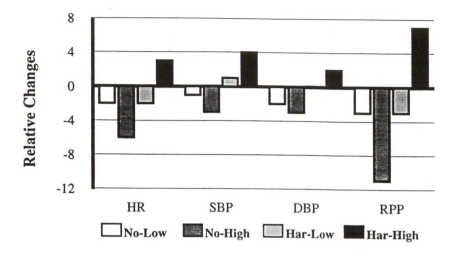

Figure 9.1. Cardiovascular responses to a mental arithmetic task under neutral conditions and conditions of harassment for high- and low-hostile men. Bars show responses as percent changes relative to the responses to an earlier task administered under nonharassing conditions. Note that only the high-hostile men consistently produced larger responses to the harassment.

NOTE: HR = Heart Rate; SBP = Systolic Blood Pressure; DBP = Diastolic Blood Pressure; RPP = Rate Pressure Product.

had consistently greater responses to the second task in the harassment condition. The *rate pressure product* (heart rate × systolic blood pressure) is a simple measure of oxygen demand by the heart muscle that indexes the workload the heart is under at the time of measurement. The responses of the harassed subjects did not diminish to the second task, and in fact increased for the highly hostile subjects.

The high-hostile subjects evaluated the situation within a hostile scheme, produced feelings of anger, and then elevated their level of sympathetically mediated cardiovascular activation. I speculate that these autonomic response differences were derived ultimately from emotion-related differences in prefrontal-hippocampal-amygdala activity in relation to the harassment. These in turn may have resulted in greater hypothalamic activation, and therefore responses of brainstem cardiovascular control centers.

Still other work shows that habitual differences in hostility may relate to differences in lipid metabolism. Engbretson and Stoney (1993) found that persons high in cynical hostility measured by the Cook and Medley hostility scale have slower metabolism of triglycerides, suggesting longer periods of blood lipid elevation after a fatty meal. This indicates that biases in situational evaluations and emotions may predict health-related alterations in lipoprotein transport and activity.

In this section, I have reviewed both neurophysiological and psychophysiological evidence that persons may differ in how they appraise situations and form emotional reactions to them. These examples suggest that individual differences at the highest levels of cortical function may determine how persons react physiologically to social situations.

There is other evidence that persons who have similar emotional response tendencies nevertheless respond differently to stress, and I suspect that these individual differences are hypothalamic in origin.

Individual Differences in Autonomic and Endocrine Reactivity to Stressor Challenge

In addition to personality factors and their effects on evaluations and emotions, hypothalamic and brainstem areas could account for differences in stress response among persons. Recent research on cardiovascular reactivity provides a useful example for a consideration of such physiologically based differences in stress responses.

Cardiovascular Reactivity

There are considerable individual differences in the magnitude of heart rate changes to mentally demanding tasks, leading to speculation that persons having consistently larger responses may be at higher risk of coronary artery disease and hypertension (Sherwood & Turner, 1992). Manuck and colleagues (Manuck & Garland, 1980) found that persons who had large heart rate rises in response to a cognitively challenging task had similarly large responses to the same task and to a different cognitive task when retested 13 months later. This made it possible to consider heart rate reactivity a stable individual difference, somewhat like a personality trait. Heart rate reactivity is also stable across different types of tasks, such as cold pressor and reaction time tests conducted 2 weeks to 13 months apart (Lovallo, Pincomb, & Wilson, 1986a) and across public speaking and mental arithmetic tasks 3 weeks apart (Sgoutas-Emch et al., 1994), again reinforcing its trait-like qualities. This stability over time and across situations provides a basis to consider reactivity tendencies as capable of affecting health. The idea that persistently large cardiovascular responses may themselves be a disease risk is known as the *cardiovascular reactivity hypothesis.*

Persons who tend to respond to stress with relatively large heart rate and blood pressure increases appear to have elevated levels of sympathetic outflow from brainstem cardiovascular control centers. I discussed autonomic controls on cardiovascular function in Chapters 4 and 5. Greater detail is provided by Cacioppo and colleagues (Berntson, Cacioppo, & Quigley, 1993, 1994; Cacioppo et al., 1994; Cacioppo, Uchino, & Berntson, 1994), who provide an extensive account of measures reflecting sympathetic and parasympathetic influences on the heart.

In considering the possible sources of individual differences in heart rate reactivity, refer to Figure 6.3. Persons who are more reactive could be more responsive at the level of the brainstem cardiovascular control nuclei, at the level of the paraventricular nucleus of the hypothalamus, at the level of the HACER, or at the emotion-producing centers of the frontal and temporal cortices. There is no strong evidence presently existing that would allow us to separate these sources of differences in response magnitude. There are reasons to speculate that differences in heart rate reactivity arise at the level of the hypothalamus, however.

My colleagues and I (Lovallo, Pincomb, & Wilson, 1986a, 1986b) tested subjects using a painful cold pressor test to stimulate heart rate responses for the purpose of heart rate reactivity classification and tested these subjects on reaction time tasks using either threat of electric shock or monetary rewards as motivation. These studies show that persons who had large heart rate increases (19 beats per minute or more) to the cold pressor test also had the largest heart rate changes to the reaction time task, regardless of the nature of the incentive. The cardiovascular reactivity groups did not differ in their perceptions or evaluations of the tasks, however. Overall, subjects in the shock avoidance study rated that task as much more aversive than the other subjects rated the rewarded task. Within each study, however, the high heart rate reactors did not report feeling more activated or distressed than their less reactive counterparts during either task (Lovallo, Pincomb, Brackett, & Wilson, 1990).

Because the heart rate response groups did not have different subjective experiences, I suspect that their cardiovascular response differences did not result from differences in how they evaluated the tasks and formed emotional reactions. Instead, it appears that the response difference was based on activational differences lower in the system.

Integrated Cardiac and Endocrine Reactivity

We reexamined the data from our studies on the aversive and rewarded versions of the reaction time task for evidence of the relationship between heart rate reactivity and cortisol responses (Lovallo et al., 1990). We compared cortisol and norepinephrine responses in high and low heart rate reactive men during the two versions of the task in a combined analysis. We expected to see greater norepinephrine responses in high heart rate reactors to both tasks and to see greater cortisol responses in this group, but only to the aversive tasks. This prediction was based on a theory that cortisol is secreted preferentially in aversive situations evoking negative emotions (Lundberg & Frankenhaeuser, 1980).

The data are displayed in Figure 9.2. First, we found that the low heart rate reactors showed little or no change in either cortisol or norepinephrine to either task. Second, the high heart rate reactors produced significant cortisol rises to the aversive task, but not to the rewarded task. They also had larger norepinephrine responses to both tasks, indicating greater global sympathetic activation. Therefore, the tendency to produce large sympathetically mediated cardiac responses appears tied to cortisol activation under conditions evoking negative emotions.

One implication of this result is that cardiovascular reactivity may relate mechanistically to adrenocortical reactivity, and therefore to modulation of the immune system. Cacioppo and colleagues (Sgoutas-Emch et al., 1994) have similarly shown that high heart rate reactors produce larger cortisol responses to mental arithmetic stress. A second implication is that negative mood states may have a disproportionate influence in highly reactive persons.

These results show that physiologically reactive persons may produce integrated patterns of both sympathetic and pituitary-adrenal activation. This suggests that the basis of this elevated reactivity must be integrated at a level higher than the brainstem and pituitary, as discussed below.

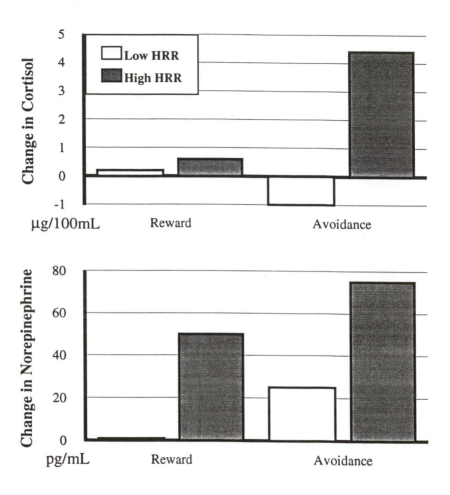

Figure 9.2. Cortisol and norepinephrine responses to reaction time tasks under conditions of reward or shock avoidance in men known to be high or low in heart rate reactivity (HRR). The high reactors had greater norepinephrine responses to both tasks, indicating greater overall sympathetic activation. The high reactors also had greater cortisol responses to the aversive task, indicating an association between heart rate reactivity and cortisol reactivity to conditions favoring cortisol secretion, such as negative emotions to the aversive task.

Central Nervous System Activity in Relation to Cardiovascular and Endocrine Reactivity

The studies reviewed above result in two major conclusions. First, high and low heart rate reactors appear to experience challenging events in the same way, suggesting that they are not differentially reactive because of differences in evaluations of the situation or the resulting emotions. Second, the tendency for large heart rate responses to be accompanied by large cortisol responses suggests that this individual difference in stress reactivity is organized at a level above the separate output pathways for autonomic and endocrine outflow. This leads me to focus on the hypothalamus as the structure most capable of producing this integrated response pattern. Whether the difference is at the level of the HACER or portions of the hypothalamus that communicate more directly with the pituitary and brainstem, such as the paraventricular nucleus, is not clear from these data; however, the pattern of results is consistent with a focus on the hypothalamus.

This line of reasoning leads to the picture of heart rate reactivity as resulting from differences among persons in the amount of hypothalamic amplification of signals arriving from evaluative and emotion-producing centers of the brain. The presumed amplification difference may therefore result in consistent individual differences in integrated autonomic and endocrine outflow, accounting for the differences between subjects in both heart rate and cortisol responses.

Health Outcomes Related to Cardiovascular and Endocrine Response Tendencies

Data suggest that long-term exposure to stress, and presumably prolonged, frequent sympathetic activation, may lead to increased rates of disease (see Lovallo & Wilson, 1992, for a review). For example, air traffic controllers working in high-workload control centers show a higher prevalence of hypertension than those working in low-volume centers (Cobb & Rose, 1973). Presumably, the long-term stress of such employment elicits greater rates of hypertension among hypertension-prone workers. In an innovative study (Timio et al., 1988), Italian nuns living in a cloistered convent were found to have no increase in blood pressure over 20 years. By comparison, control women from the surrounding community showed the typical age-related increase over the same time.

Individuals living near Three-Mile Island during the nuclear accident who believed the area was contaminated with radioactivity showed elevated urinary cortisol levels months after the event. Other evidence indicates that traumatic stress during natural disasters can produce immediate changes in health. The second greatest cause of mortality in the 1994 Los Angeles earthquake was sudden death due to heart attack. The 1989 Loma Prieta earthquake near San Francisco produced severe dissociative reactions and longer-term psychological sequelae. Other examples of the health effects of traumatic stress are discussed in Chapter 7.

These studies of stress and health suggest that we should expect the greatest future health consequences in persons having the largest sympathetic and endocrine responses. There is evidence that this is the case, both in cardiovascular disease risk and in altered immune system function. Persons may differ in how they respond to stress because of personality traits, such as hostility, or because of hypothalamically mediated differences in reactivity tendencies. I have reason to believe that both types of individual differences in response to stress can contribute uniquely to differences in health.

Personality Mediators of Risk for Premature Mortality

There are at least two lines of evidence that personality characteristics and their associated perceptions, evaluations, and emotions may have long-term health consequences. The first line of evidence concerns the effects of hopelessness on health as described in Chapter 7. Persons expressing feelings of hopelessness were at substantially increased risk of premature death due to all causes, including cardiovascular diseases, over the next several years, even though these persons were normally healthy at the start of the study (Everson, Kaplan, Goldberg, & Salonen, 1996).

The second line of evidence indicates that hostility is also a psychological contributor to negative health outcomes. Williams and colleagues (Barefoot et al., 1983) found that persons high in cynical hostility as measured by the Cook-Medley HO scale were at increased risk of death due to all causes. In light of the studies by Suarez (Suarez & Williams, 1989) and Everson (Everson et al., 1996), one may speculate that hostile persons perceive many social situations in a negative light, produce feelings of hostility, and develop exaggerated physiological responses. Such situational appraisals and their accompanying responses may be at the root of the elevated death rates seen in highly hostile persons. At present no data exist on the physiological response tendencies of hopeless persons, and therefore we do not have an equally plausible hypothesis for the mechanistic links involved.

Cardiovascular Reactivity as a Mediator of Disease Risk

I now turn to evidence supporting the idea that exaggerated cardiovascular response tendencies may also have negative health outcomes.

In 1932, Hines and Brown were interested in predicting which persons were likely to develop hypertension in the future (Lovallo, 1975). They reasoned that because hypertensive persons have large blood pressure responses to stress, normotensive persons who spontaneously show large responses may in turn be at high risk of hypertension. This early version of the reactivity hypothesis was based on the psychosomatic idea that exaggerated responses to stress were evidence of a flaw in the cardiovascular systems of highly reactive persons, and that this flaw might ultimately result in essential hypertension (see Alexander, 1950). More generally, a basic assumption of the theory relating stress to disease risk is that the sympathetic nervous system and accompanying endocrine reactions can exert damaging effects on the body when responses are frequent and of large magnitude. Evidence has slowly accumulated suggesting that exaggerated cardiovascular reactivity in fact does predict greater risk of future cardiovascular disease.

Among monkeys living in social groups, the highly reactive individuals are at greatest risk for heart disease. Manuck and colleagues (Manuck, Kaplan, Adams, & Clarkson, 1989) tested monkeys' heart rate responses by approaching their group living quarters wearing a large "monkey glove," indicating that one of the monkeys was about to be captured for some sort of procedure. Monkeys view this as a substantial stressor, and the heart rate responses may be presumed to accompany negative emotions and evaluations of threat. Several years later, the monkeys were sacrificed to examine their coronary arteries for atherosclerosis. The highly reactive monkeys had more extensive areas of atherosclerotic disease and greater progression of their lesions. Interestingly, this effect could be eliminated by beta blockers, indicating that reduction of the cardiac responses or related emotions could improve health outcomes in the highly reactive monkeys.

There is also suggestive evidence that large cardiovascular responses to stress indicate greater risk of hypertension in later years. The first line of work shows that normotensive young men at high risk for hypertension, based on family history and moderately elevated systolic blood pressures, have the largest blood pressure responses to mental arithmetic stress (al'Absi, Everson, & Lovallo, 1995; Everson, Lovallo, Sausen, & Wilson, 1992). These results are consistent with the reactivity hypothesis, namely, that the greater reactivity of the high-risk persons is either a marker of greater hypertension risk or it contributes in a causal way.

The second line of work relates greater cardiovascular stress responses to increased rates of hypertension in later years, as originally predicted by Hines and Brown. Persons with the largest blood pressure responses to cold pressor stimulation had the greatest cumulative incidence of hypertension 30 years later (Menkes et al., 1989). Men with the highest systolic blood pressures during a reaction time task using electric shock as the incentive had the highest blood pressures 10-15 years later (Light, Sherwood, & Turner, 1992). Everson and colleagues (Everson et al., 1996a) have shown that men having the largest blood pressure rises in anticipation of a bicycle exercise stress test had the greatest prevalence of hypertension 4 years later. The blood pressures seen prior to exercise are affected by mental activity associated with preparation for a severe bout of exertion, as noted in Chapter 5. In a related vein, elevated cardiovascular reactivity to mental stressors is related to elevations in blood levels of low-density lipoprotein cholesterol, a significant risk factor for coronary heart disease (Fredrikson, Lundberg, & Tuomisto, 1991).

Immune System Alterations, Cardiovascular Reactivity, and Health

In Chapter 8, I noted that both sympathetic activity and cortisol secretion are important modulators of immune function. One should therefore expect that persons having the greatest responses to stress will have the greatest modulation of immune system function. The studies reviewed earlier indicated that heart rate responses to mental stress are related both to greater evidence of global sympathetic activation and to greater cortisol secretion to appropriate situational cues, strengthening this contention. In fact, recent work suggests that sympathetically mediated cardiac responses to stressors such as mental arithmetic and public speaking are also related to alterations in indicators of immune system function. Cacioppo and colleagues (Sgoutas-Emch et al., 1994) preselected high and low heart rate reactive men based on reactions to a speech stressor, during which the low reactors showed a heart rate response of +5 beats per minute (bpm) and the high reactors showed a heart rate response of +30 bpm. Three weeks later, these reactivity groups were retested on a mental arithmetic challenge. As expected, the high heart reactors showed larger heart rate and blood pressure responses to the mental arithmetic tasks, and they had larger cortisol responses. The highly reactive subjects had the greatest increases in natural killer cell activation, indexed by the ability of their natural killer cells to attack and kill infected cells in a laboratory assay. Note that this greater reactivity tendency was associated in this brief stressor with enhanced cortisol responses and enhanced immune function, not with depressed immune function. I suspect that this is an example of the ability of cortisol and sympathetic activity to increase immune system function in response to mild stressors of brief duration.

Indeed, other work suggests that cortisol reactivity predicts depressed immune function as indicated by reactivation of latent viral infection (Cacioppo et al., 1995). Elderly women and female undergraduates worked on a combination of mental arithmetic and a speech stressor. Women with the largest cortisol responses had the greatest evidence of latent virus reactivation as indicated by their higher antibody titers to the Epstein-Barr virus. The higher viral titers in the more reactive women are considered an indicator of recent reactivation of the virus, thus suggesting a decrease in immune system surveillance of this normally latent virus.

The overall pattern of these results shows that autonomic function, endocrine function, and immune system function are linked in states of stress. This pattern shows a significant degree of individual variation, leading to the conclusion that individuals differ in centrally determined autonomic responsivity and that such differences can potentially have consequences on immune system function and presumably on long-term health. Clearly, much work remains to be done in this intriguing area.

▓ Discussion

The emergence of an integrated field of study incorporating neurophysiology, personality theory, autonomic and endocrine function, immune system activity, and health provides a powerful set of tools, permitting a multilevel approach to the understanding of health and disease. The information reviewed above leads to the consideration that systematic relationships may exist between the tendency of some persons to be highly reactive to stress and to suffer more negative health consequences. I have attempted to systematize disparate lines of research using the model of centrally determined stress responses presented in Chapter 6. This allows a top-to-bottom integration of how the system could be altered by what we think and feel; in turn, these tendencies to think and feel in certain ways may have a strong biological and experiential basis. Ultimately, physiological behaviors accompanying evaluations and emotions become major influences on our bodies.

I presented evidence that individual differences in stress response can arise out of differences in situational appraisals and differences in resulting emotional responses, pointing to activity in prefrontal and temporal structures. I presented other evidence that response biases can be determined by activational differences at the hypothalamus. I then presented evidence that both psychologically and physiologically based reactivity differences could result in impaired health.

The ultimate value of attempting to integrate information on evaluative processes, emotions, and autonomic-endocrine outflow into models of disease etiology is twofold. First, we will be able to view health and disease as the outcome of psychophysiological processes encompassing both the behavior and the physiology of the individual. Second, the individual-differences approach described here helps us understand more clearly the mechanisms relating behavior to health and disease, and it provides ways to identify persons at greatest risk of disease.

Returning to the basic question concerning how ideas can come to have power over our bodies, one can see that meaningful relationships among evaluations, mood states, and central nervous system function exist in relation to emotion tendencies. These in turn determine autonomic and endocrine outflow. The evidence reviewed here suggests that there are indeed systematic differences among persons and their reactions to psychological stressors. These differences translate into consistent differences in endocrine effects on the immune system and autonomic alterations on cardiovascular structures. But the list of targets for such peripheral changes, limited to immune and cardiovascular functions, is not complete. These two classes of outcomes are the best studied to date, and they fit neatly into the framework of this book. But there is reason to believe that individual differences in psychological stress response and health consequences are not limited to the influences of cardiovascular reactions and adrenocortical responses. There are likely to be other mechanistic relationships among differences in the activity of the central nervous system and health.

SUMMARY

In this chapter, I reviewed evidence that persons may have different ways of responding to potential threats. Persons may differ systematically in how they perceive and evaluate situations they face. These differences may determine consistent differences in emotional responses. For example, persons having strongly negative emotions to a variety of situations are likely to have greater autonomically mediated cardiovascular reactions, even ones inappropriate to the situation at hand. Persons may also differ in their hypothalamic and brainstem activational tendencies, even when they do not differ in their perceptions and emotional reactions. Research on persons with greater heart rate responses shows that there is considerable stability of such responses across situations and over time. Whether the source of exaggerated physiological activation is an emotional response bias, such as trait hostility, or an autonomic response bias, the exaggerated reactivity has the same effect on the periphery, expressed as larger autonomic and endocrine reactions. These individual differences in stress reactivity have their origins in inborn response dispositions and differences in experience. There is increasing evidence that differences in stress reactivity predict differences in health outcomes. More generally, they indicate that the ways in which ideas can influence the body can vary systematically from person to person and become major predictors of health and disease.

FURTHER READING

Manuck, S. B., Kasprowicz, A. L., & Muldoon, M. F. (1990). Behaviorally evoked cardiovascular reactivity and hypertension: Conceptual issues and potential associations. *Annals of Behavioral Medicine, 12,* 17-29.

This provides a brief discussion of issues concerning cardiovascular reactivity and hypertension.

Turner, J. R. (1994). *Cardiovascular reactivity and stress: Patterns of physiological response.* New York: Plenum.

This volume is a very thorough coverage of cardiovascular reactivity research in relation to individual differences.

Turner, J. R., Sherwood, A., & Light, K. C. (Eds.). *Individual differences in cardiovascular response to stress.* New York: Plenum.

This is an extended discussion of individual differences in stress reactivity, including factors not dealt with here, such as reactivity differences due to gender and race. The chapters by Lovallo and Wilson also describe how peripheral factors in the development of hypertension can contribute to exaggerated blood pressure reactivity to stress.

Behavior, Stress, and Health

At the beginning of this book, I posed the question: How can ideas come to have power over our bodies? From the point of a truly behavioral medicine, we need to understand how all our behaviors, including our thoughts and emotions, can alter our physical selves. As I have tried to show, the study of psychological stress is perfectly suited to this task because it forces us to consider how our perceptions and interpretations of the world can result in negative emotions and how these can change the autonomic and endocrine influences on the rest of the body.

The Historical Dilemma of Mind-Body Dualism

I have addressed the mind-body relationship and the concept of psychological stress from a historical perspective. Mind-body dualism limits how we think about ourselves, and it limits our science of biology and medicine. Our dualistic view makes it impossible for us to understand how the apparently nonphysical thoughts that occupy our heads come to have influence over our bodies. As a result, we have had a very difficult time in developing a framework for medicine that incorporates behavior, both as a cause and as a cure.

I contrasted traditional biomedicine with an emerging theoretical framework for behavioral medicine. I argued that because of our adherence to a dualistic view of mind and body, the development of a mechanistic physiology and neurophysiology has excluded our experiential, evaluative, goal-directed existence from our biology. As a result, we lack ways to model how thoughts may affect health, and this in turn has hindered the development of a behavioral medicine.

Behavioral medicine calls for removal of the metaphysical dichotomy between mind and body. It calls for us to theorize properly about the influence of perceptions, thoughts, and emotions on biology. Ultimately, it may allow us to consider social processes and culture as causal agents in health and disease. The advantage of this behavioral agenda for medicine is that we may then develop mechanistically rigorous theories that allow for behavioral causes as well as behavioral treatments of disease.

The starting point for this effort seems to lie in how psychologists conceptualize cognitive processes in relation to brain function. Some cognitive approaches based on computer metaphors continue to separate the mysterious software of the mind from the concrete hardware of the brain. The problem with this view is that the software has a separate existence from the hardware in our computers. The software runs on the hardware without altering it. This computer metaphor fails to help us appreciate how the operation of our thoughts and emotions is completely at one with the neurophysiological behavior of our brains.

Instead, our thoughts are a fundamental expression of the behavior of our brain, and it is not possible for us to have thoughts and feelings that do not involve changes in our brain. This recognition has been slow in coming, however, and forming a tight linkage between neural events and behaviors has a remarkably short history in the study of behavior. For example, the first known relationship between a behavior and a definable neuronal event did not occur until 1969, when Slangen and Miller reported that norepinephrine released by nerve terminals in the hypothalamus elicited eating behavior in rats (see Miller, 1995).

▓ Matter and Behavior

Although space limits my ability to deal with the mind-body problem in depth, I will briefly consider why it is unhelpful to view our mental activities in terms of the Cartesian "ghost in the machine." I will also propose a solution: that all matter, by nature, is continually interactive with both energy forces and other matter. By extension, it is fundamentally contradictory to devise special rules to guide the behavior of matter that is organized biologically. Considering our human psychology, this unitary principle is not contradicted by our self-awareness and our ability to talk about ourselves in books such as this one.

As I noted in Chapter 1, Descartes (1637/1956) imagines the body without the soul to be an inert entity. This view was part of the generally held 17th-century attitude that all matter was fundamentally inert. Ferguson said, "That matter can never put itself in motion is allowed by all men" (cited in Toulmin, 1967, p. 823). In fact, Isaac Newton argued that matter could only react to direct pressure or contact from *other matter* outside itself. The same matter and energy distinction was considered true for living things. Anticipating the vitalists who antagonized Bernard in the 19th century, Borelli argued 200 years earlier that muscles are passive organs that could move the limbs only when acted on by the "motive faculty of the soul" (cited in Toulmin, 1967, p. 824).

The view that matter was inert was later opposed by a small minority of writers such as Mettrie (Toulmin, 1967), who argued that matter was not fundamentally unmoving but was in fact inherently active. Like Mettrie, I argue that matter is not inert and that our consciousness proceeds naturally from our biology. Consciousness should be seen as a result of the elementary structure of our central nervous system in relation to its higher-order organization. To clarify the relationship between structure and function in the nervous system, consider Mettrie's idea using some simple examples.

As Toulmin (1967) points out, physics long ago abandoned the Newtonian idea that matter consists of otherwise inactive particles colliding only when acted on by some outside force. This older style of physics views material states and energy processes as fundamentally separate things. In contrast, for the past 100 years, matter has been seen by physics as constantly interacting with itself. Using a term from psychology, matter is fundamentally *behaving.* Considering matter at its most elementary level, this view applies in describing the structure-function of quarks, the candidates for the fundamental constituents of matter. I use the term *structure-function* here because the mathematical description of quarks includes both their energetic behavior and their physical properties in a single descriptive phrase. Quarks have the properties of charge, charm, and color. Each of these properties expresses not a fixed aspect of the quark's physical makeup but consistent rules for the quark's behavior in relation to physical properties. For quarks, their material properties and their behaviors are inseparable. The same statements hold true for more complex particles such as protons and neutrons and for atoms and molecules, even though the rules specifying structure and behavior become extraordinarily complex at this level.

What holds for simpler particles also holds true for more complex constructions of matter.

What about biology? If I agree that biological material is constructed of the same simple stuff that makes up all material things, I can begin to see that the distinction between biological material things and nonbiological material things is already arbitrary. I can then make the same series of arguments here. Namely, the structure of biological entities determines that they behave in accordance with their structure and that more complex biological entities are accordingly capable of increasingly greater ranges of behavior.

I may start by considering the behavior of a simple biological entity, the sodium channel. Found on virtually all lipid membranes in the body, the sodium channel is responsible for keeping most of the sodium outside our neurons and opening on command to allow sodium to enter in the process of a nerve firing. Figure 10.1 is an illustration of the sodium channel as we now know it. The sodium channel starts as a particular sequence of amino acids that form themselves into a long protein molecule. With the help of chaperon proteins, these 1-dimensional strings of amino acids fold up on themselves in complex ways to form 3-dimensional protein molecules. Sodium channels have a unique 3-dimensional shape that is a direct result of the specific sequence of amino acids in the original chain. The completed protein has new behavioral capabilities that are a direct result of its emergent 3-dimensional structure. A sodium channel, in its lipid membrane, can change shape in predictable ways given specific stimuli in its microenvironment. The channels have a central pore through which sodium ions may pass, and the pore has a series of gates that keep sodium ions out and let them in on command. It has specific external domains that respond to the environment

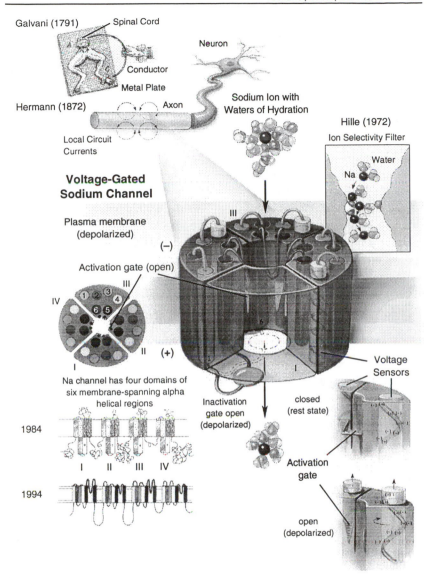

Figure 10.1. The relationship between structure and function in the sodium channel. The 3-dimensional amino acid chain winds through the lipid membrane of the neuron to form four domains, creating a central pore capable of regulating the flow of sodium ions across the membrane using a series of four molecular gates. The actions of the gates are controlled by voltage-sensitive segments of the molecule that alter the state of the gates.

to increase or decrease the neuron's resting potential and the strength of its discharge.

In recognition of the relationship between structure and function, neurobiologists study the behavior of the channel by altering its structure in known ways and examining the resulting changes in function. Such investigation tells us how the internal gates work to regulate ion flow. It helps us see how sodium ions are able to tumble through the pore itself. The success of this research agenda leads to the conclusion that the functioning of the sodium channel is inseparable from its structure and any change in the physical makeup of the original amino acid chain must produce a reliable change in how the molecule functions. As in the case of quarks, the behavior of the sodium channel is determined by its structure, even though the sodium channel is orders of magnitude more complex than a quark.

Because a sodium channel is far simpler than a brain, it is perhaps easier to grasp intuitively how the amino acid structure of the channel determines its behavior. In the case of an entire brain, the argument may have less intuitive appeal, and there is no simple substitute to prove the case. In Chapters 1 and 2, however, I noted that science is grounded on the premise that the rules describing the behavior of simple things are fundamentally the same as the rules for complex things. That is, the world does not acquire categorically (ontologically) new entities by virtue of things becoming structurally more complex. By extension, the rules guiding structure-function relationships should hold for complex combinations of neurons and for whole brains just as they hold for the far simpler sodium channels.

This is not to underestimate the difficulties in forming useful models of neural structures and their related functions. For example, in the case of the sodium channel, science has been inquiring into the conduction of nerve impulses for more than 250 years. The study of whole brains will certainly take a long time. In spite of these empirical and conceptual difficulties, the willingness to examine behavior and biology in a unified way will continue to provide useful insights, including the effect of mental activity on the structure of the brain.

As a step in this direction, it is now possible to relate changes in brain activity to the subject's performance of specific cognitive tasks (see Kosslyn & Koenig, 1995) and his or her experience of given emotional states. But can the behavior of the system also change its biology? Recent studies suggest clearly that it can. Patients undergoing 10 weeks of cognitive-behavioral therapy for obsessive-compulsive disorder were shown to have changes in limbic system activity as measured noninvasively by positron emission tomography (Schwartz, Stoessel, Baxter, Martin, & Phelps, 1996). The observed changes mimicked those produced by pharmacological treatment for the same disorder. Similar behavioral effects on neural systems are seen in studies of behavioral dominance in crayfish (Barinaga, 1996). When pairs of crayfish fight to establish dominance, the winner begins to secrete more serotonin and the loser secretes less. The serotonin primes the nervous system of the dominant crayfish to function more effectively in aggressive behaviors. This is another example of the effect of behavior on the long-term state of the nervous system and the ultimate elicitation of new or altered behaviors. These changed behaviors will affect the nervous system in new ways, with yet further consequences for behavior. These examples of behavioral-structural interactions provide evidence that the principles guiding the study of emotions and behaviors need not be fundamentally different from the language used to describe our physiological states and processes. Such evidence suggests that psychological stressors and their related emotions may well affect our brains and our bodies.

Although this recognition is fundamental to resolving the paradox of mind and body, it does not answer the most difficult questions, such as how the organized behavior of collections of neurons ultimately becomes our subjective experience or how our sense of self-continuity over time arises from this neuronal activity. A number of highly creative approaches are being taken to these matters in the field of the neurosciences, however (see Churchland, 1986; Damasio, 1994).

Behavioral Medicine in Relation to Traditional Medicine

Moving from the broad framework of the mind-body problem, one should be equally concerned with how behavioral medicine differs from traditional medicine. Our views of health, disease, and treatment are strongly influenced by the models used to describe these processes. In Chapter 2, I considered a series of models of disease viewed within a traditional framework of biomedicine and then described how these would differ within a conceptually broader behavioral medicine perspective. The key distinction between these two views is that in a behavioral medicine, it becomes permissible to think about how conscious processes can have causal agency in the body. This in turn allows us to think about the possibility that social and even cultural processes can affect health.

This shift from a view of the body as a passive agent, acted on by a pathogen or a treatment, to an active entity that takes in information, evaluates it, and reacts to those evaluations not only opens up new ways of thinking about what makes us sick but also permits new ways of thinking about what can make us well (see Foss & Rothenberg, 1988).

To focus these broad questions onto the narrower topic of this book, I introduced in Chapter 3 a history of the concept of stress. This historical description allows us to see the roots of the Cartesian dilemma in the current model of biology. Notably, Bernard (1865/1961) had to contend with the antimechanistic vitalists then active in French intellectual circles. Because the vitalists argued that the body was acted on internally by a nonphysical vital force, Bernard was compelled to argue against this physiological version of the ghost in the machine and to assert a mechanistic epistemology for the science of physiology. This effort successfully established the basis for considering lawful physical relationships in traditional physiology, but it did not readily give us a way to think about how psychological events could alter brain and bodily function. Ironically, the Cartesian dualism persisted in our thinking about the workings of the mind even after the mysterious vital forces had been banished from the working of the rest of the body. Partly for this reason, modern medicine has not incorporated behavior into its conceptual framework.

The consideration of physical and psychological stress provides one way to think about the relationship between psychological events and physiological events in the body. I have proposed in this book that laying down a mechanistic model of physical stress leads more naturally to an understanding of how psychological events can also come to act as stressors.

▓ Systems Organization and Stress

In Chapter 4, I described the normal modes of bodily regulation to consider the disruptions caused by psychological stress. I noted that homeostatic regulation involves layers of control over each organ and tissue, starting with the local regulation designed into each of these and proceeding to increasingly elaborate levels of nervous system and hormonal regulation, up to and including the functions of the hypothalamus. Higher levels in the system therefore modulate and coordinate the activity of lower levels.

I then discussed in Chapter 5 the admittedly arbitrary distinction between physiological and psychological stressors. I noted that in both cases, common output pathways and peripheral mechanisms are engaged. The essential difference is that in physiological stress, exemplified by exercise stress, the major sources of perturbation to the system are the metabolic demands on fuel homeostasis and feedback from working muscles, with the added influence of mental effort. In the case of psychological stressors, the major sources of perturbation are descending influences originating in higher brain centers and operating without regard to physiological demands (see Turner & Carroll, 1985).

Chapter 6 forms the focal point of this book. I described how the central nervous system is equipped to carry out a continuous monitoring of the environment and prepares constantly to make adaptive responses. This process is associated with a continual flow of emotional experience and resulting physiological outputs. Psychologically, the generation of emotions may occur to present threats or to imagined, remembered, and anticipated threats. The frontal cortex appears to mediate working memory. Working memory is able to produce a realistic representation of events, including those that are not actually present. The prefrontal cortex, in its relationship to the limbic system, operates on processes typically considered purely psychological in nature—ideas, perceptions, and memories. In response to these imagined or recalled events, we produce the same stream of emotions and their related autonomic and endocrine outputs that originally evolved to deal with immediate physical threats. This model provides one answer to the basic question of how ideas could come to have power over our bodies.

The layered organization of the system, with local metabolic controls at the bottom and ganglionic and spinal reflexes, brainstem reflexes, hypothalamic regulation, and ultimately cortical and limbic controls at the top, allows us to think about how cortical activity associated with evaluations and emotions can alter the functioning of the lower levels. Conceived of in this way, the cortex applies the highest level of control to the regulation of bodily processes. In the context of a model of psychological stress, we can therefore think about how mental states can produce fight-flight responses in the body.

I also noted that the distinction between physical and psychological stress was really arbitrary because all physical stressors have a psychological component in a conscious person. For this reason, there may be no such thing as a pure physical stressor, although there may be pure psychological stressors.

▓ Psychological Stress and Its Consequences

With the model described in Chapter 6, I was then able to discuss the consequences of psychological stress. In Chapter 7, I dealt with the severe, even disastrous, effects that feelings of complete helplessness can engender in humans and laboratory animals. I discussed examples from anthropological observation of persons dying as an apparent result of witchcraft; closer to our own experience, I gave examples of death due to the psychological experience of fear and helplessness in the face of wars and natural disasters. Although these are dramatic demonstrations of psychological effects on health, they are far removed from everyday experience and are extreme relative to more chronic psychological stress experienced on a daily basis.

I then turned to a series of animal studies on the influences of coping and control over aversive events. These provide an excellent basis for understanding some key physiological causes of the body's response to psychological stress. These studies illustrate graphically that removal of adequate coping options during exposure to aversive stimulation can result in severe physical consequences in the form of ulcers and other tissue pathology. Most interesting, these effects are paralleled by changes in central nervous system noradrenergic and serotonergic transmitter systems. These changes in turn produce behavioral manifestations of mood disorders such as depression. Returning to the Lazarus model of psychological stress, I noted that coping and control in the face of aversive threats are the major determinants of psychologically induced stress responses. Similarly, reducing the experience of helplessness can powerfully avert the psychophysiological consequences of the physical stressor.

In Chapter 8, I showed how psychological processes and immune system function are linked. I was able to draw from a variety of creative studies that have capitalized on naturally occurring stressors to measure changes in immune system functions in persons' daily lives. Such work is relevant to the human condition, and it provides an increasingly clear view of the effect of psychological events on health. This work tends to be correlational in nature, matching up immune system changes with experience of lack of control or ceaseless struggle in daily life. What remains is to understand how the causal chain of events operates from the experience of life to altered emotions, limbic system function, and altered hypothalamic and autonomic function. Most important, we need to know much more about how practical, minimally invasive measures of immune system function can be used to reflect actual disease susceptibility.

In Chapter 9, I showed how individual differences in psychological processes, such as hostile interpretations of social interactions, and the resulting emotions, can increase the size of cardiovascular reactions to those interactions. In considering the relationships among behavioral dispositions, external circumstances, stress, and health, one is always impressed by the enormous differences among persons in how they cope with and react to life's challenges. A complete model of psychological stress and health will have much to say about how these individual differences arise and how they determine the nature of the person's interactions with the environment. In addition to telling us much about stress and disease, they promise to tell us even more about how persons may be highly flexible in absorbing life's challenges and avoiding their worst consequences.

Stress and Behavioral Medicine

The lessons about the negative effects of stress on health are potentially useful in helping us understand restorative processes and think about how mental activity may exert beneficial physical effects. Returning for a moment to the earlier example about the effects of psychotherapy on brain function, I presume that the altered brain activity would be accompanied by altered influences of the brain on the rest of the body.

If emotions associated with psychological stress can produce stress hormone secretion and increased sympathetic activation along with all the related physiological changes, it seems reasonable to argue that the opposite could occur. In a similar fashion, one may ask what untapped sources exist for behavioral therapies and interventions in acute and chronic disease. In Chapter 8, I alluded to some possibilities, including Spiegel's behavioral intervention in women with breast cancer (Spiegel et al., 1989). The validity of such approaches remains to be proven; until the evidence is in, a healthy skepticism should prevail. But skepticism does not mean that the effort to explore the possibilities should not be made, only that we should pursue the agenda of behavioral medicine from a rigorously scientific perspective and be cautious about the results. The potential is to increase our understanding of the ways in which we interact with our world and in how these interactions can affect us for better or worse.

▓ Psychological Stress and Its Bodily Effects

In considering the effects of psychological stress and possible health consequences, we tend to focus on the effects of autonomic outflow and endocrine secretions on peripheral organs. For example, we think of the effects on the development of heart disease through its effects on cardiovascular activation or epinephrine secretion, as discussed in Chapter 9. Similarly, we think of stress as affecting the operation of the immune system and reducing resistance to infectious disease. These are certainly important ways in which stress mechanisms interact with organ regulation to alter homeostasis. As we learn more about the brain mechanisms integrating the psychological stress response, however, we realize that psychological stress is likely to have important consequences for brain function.

The model in Chapter 6 illustrates that psychological stress is a result of activity arising in the prefrontal and limbic regions and altering the functioning of the hypothalamus and brainstem autonomic control centers. The system appears to be functionally integrated by the system of corticotropin releasing factor neurons and to involve altered activation and dysphoric moods associated with the noradrenergic fiber system and the serotonergic system. The studies of uncontrollable stress in rats indicate that altered central nervous system function is a prominent consequence of severe psychological stress. I speculated in Chapter 7 that long-lasting changes in the response tendencies of the central nervous system areas integrating the psychological stress response may be responsible for the long-term changes associated with posttraumatic stress disorder. Such changes involve altered activation to novel or unexpected stimuli, mood alterations, and powerful autonomic and endocrine responses. In turn, this suggests that some of the most important effects of severe psychological stress are long-term alterations in the function of the brain.

▦ Stress, Stress Reduction, and Improved Health

Because this is a book on stress, I have paid a great deal of attention to how events can produce negative reactions in the sense that they can impair health. But because this book is part of a series on behavioral medicine, it seems appropriate to think about possibilities on the positive side of the coin. If psychological events can produce stress effects in the body, it should be in principle possible for psychological events to have beneficial effects. We have paid far too little attention to the possibilities of such salubrious influences. Although many persons are prepared to think of psychological stress as impairing health, we are less well prepared to think about positive states of mind having beneficial physical effects. The more we know about the relationships among our behaviors, including our thoughts and emotions, the more likely we are to see how mental activities can act to buffer the effects of stress and increase our resistance to its negative physical effects.

SUMMARY
▦▦▦▦▦▦▦

This chapter is a short review of the major themes of this book. The primary question is how ideas can come to have power over our bodies. I used the topic of psychological stress to show that events, thoughts, and perceptions of the world, and our evaluations of their meaning for ourselves, can come to have both immediate physical consequences and potential long-term health consequences. I focused on stress in behavioral medicine and the relationship of behavioral medicine to the larger fields of traditional medicine and biology. To lay the groundwork for understanding the relationship between behavior and health, I argued that it is necessary to stop categorizing behavior, especially psychological or mental processes, as fundamentally different from our material makeup. This artificial distinction, in the form of the mind-body problem, makes it conceptually impossible to consider properly how behavior relates to physical health.

I attempted to give a more narrowly focused neurophysiological model of that process in Chapter 6 and to give examples of the workings of that process in Chapters 7, 8, and 9. I hope that by increasing understanding of the relationships between psychological events and bodily stress responses, we will gain a greater appreciation for the relationship between behavior and health. This in turn contributes to our development of a behavioral medicine. In the largest sense, it contributes to a reframed understanding of our nature as living beings whose behavior is not separate from our physical makeup and whose health is not separate from our thoughts and emotions.

FURTHER READING

Churchland, P. S. (1986). *Neurophilosophy: Toward a unified science of the mind/brain.* Cambridge: MIT Press.

This provides an extended discussion of the issue of mind-body relationships and the need for a dialogue among the neurosciences, psychology, and philosophy to reconceptualize ourselves in a manner that does away with the Cartesian paradox.

Damasio, A. R. (1994). *Descartes' error: Emotion, reason, and the human brain.* New York: Putnam.

This brief account of the relationship between the mind and the brain is contained in a thoughtfully written last chapter.

Foss, L., & Rothenberg, K. (1988). *The second medical revolution.* Boston: Shambhala.

The beginnings of a reformulation of medicine are laid out here.

References

Ader, R., & Cohen, N. (1993). Psychoneuroimmunology: Conditioning and stress. *Annual Review of Psychology, 44*, 53-85.

al'Absi, M., Everson, S. A., & Lovallo, W. R. (1995). Hypertension risk factors and cardiovascular reactivity to mental stress in young men. *International Journal of Psychophysiology, 20*, 155-160.

al'Absi, M., Lovallo, W. R., McKey, B. S., & Pincomb, G. A. (1994). Borderline hypertensives produce exaggerated adrenocortical responses to sustained mental stress. *Psychosomatic Medicine, 56*, 245-250.

Alexander, F. (1950). *Psychosomatic medicine, its principles and applications.* New York: Norton.

Allen, M. T., Obrist, P. A., Sherwood, A., & Crowell, M. D. (1987). Evaluation of myocardial and peripheral vascular responses during reaction time, mental arithmetic and cold pressor. *Psychophysiology, 24*, 648-656.

Anderson, D. E., & Tosheff, J. G. (1973). Cardiac output and total peripheral resistance changes during pre-avoidance periods in the dog. *Journal of Applied Physiology, 35*, 650-654.

Aston-Jones, G., Ennis, M., Pieribone, R. A., Nickell, W. T., & Shipley, M. T. (1986). The brain nucleus locus coeruleus: restricted afferent control of a broad efferent network. *Science, 234*, 734-737.

Bachen, E. A., Manuck, S. B., Cohen, S., Muldoon, M. F., Raible, R., Herbert, T. B., & Rabin, B. S. (1995). Adrenergic blockade ameliorates cellular immune responses to mental stress in humans. *Psychosomatic Medicine, 57*, 366-372.

Barefoot, J. C., Dahlstrom, W. G., & Williams, R. B. (1983). Hostility, CHD incidence, and total mortality: A 25 year follow up study of 255 physicians. *Psychosomatic Medicine, 45*, 59-63.

Barinaga, M. (1996). Social status sculpts activity of crayfish neurons. *Science, 271*, 290-291.

Baum, A. (1990). Stress, intrusive imagery, and chronic distress. *Health Psychology, 9*, 653-675.

Benson, H., & McCallie, D. P., Jr. (1979). Angina pectoris and the placebo effect. *New England Journal of Medicine, 300*, 1424-1429.

Berk, L. S., Tan, S. A., Fry, W. F., Napier, B. J., Lee, J. W., Hubbard, R. W., Lewis, J. E., & Eby, J. C. (1989). Neuroendocrine and stress hormone changes during mirthful laughter. *American Journal of the Medical Sciences, 298,* 390-396.

Bernard, C. (1961). *An introduction to the study of experimental medicine* (H. C. Greene, Trans.). New York: Collier. (Original work published 1865)

Berntson, G. G., Cacioppo, J. T., & Quigley, K. S. (1993). Respiratory sinus arrhythmia: Autonomic origins, physiological mechanisms, and psychophysiological implications. *Psychophysiology, 30,* 183-196.

Berntson, G. G., Cacioppo, J. T., & Quigley, K. S. (1994). Autonomic cardiac control. I. Estimation and validation from pharmacological blockades. *Psychophysiology, 31,* 572-585.

Blum, K., Cull, H. G., Braverman, E. R., & Comings, D. E. (1996). Reward deficiency syndrome. *American Scientist, 84,* 132-145.

Bonneau, R. H. (1994). Experimental approaches to identify mechanisms of stress-induced modulation of immunity to herpes simplex virus infection. In R. Glaser & J. K. Kiecolt-Glaser (Eds.), *Handbook of human stress and immunity* (pp. 125-160). San Diego: Academic.

Booth-Kewley, S., & Friedman, H. (1987). Psychological predictors of heart disease: A quantitative review. *Psychological Bulletin, 101,* 343-362.

Brady, J. R. (1973). Personal control over aversive stimuli and its relation to stress. *Psychological Bulletin, 80,* 286-303.

Brady, J. V. (1955). Ulcers in "executive" monkeys. *Scientific American, 199*(4), 95-100.

Brady, J. V., Porter, R. W., Conrad, D. G., & Mason, J. W. (1958). Avoidance behavior and the development of gastroduodenal ulcers. *Journal of the Experimental Analysis of Behavior, 1,* 69-72.

Brod, J. (1963). Hemodynamic basis of acute pressor reactions and hypertension. *British Heart Journal, 25,* 227-245.

Brown, G. L., Goodwin, F. K., Ballenger, J. C., Goyer, P. F., & Major, L. F. (1986). Aggression in humans correlates with cerebrospinal fluid amine metabolites. *Annals of the New York Academy of Sciences, 487,* 176-188.

Cacioppo, J.T. (in press). Somatic responses to psychological stress: The reactivity hypothesis. *Advances in Psychological Science, Vol. 2.*

Cacioppo, J. T., & Berntson, G. G. (1994). Relationship between attitudes and evaluative space: A critical review, with emphasis on the separability of positive and negative substrates. *Psychological Bulletin, 115,* 401-423.

Cacioppo, J. T., Berntson, G. G., Binkley, P. F., Quigley, L. S., Uchino, B. N., & Fieldstone, A. (1994). Autonomic cardiac control: II. Noninvasive indices and basal response as revealed by autonomic blockades. *Psychophysiology, 31,* 586-598.

Cacioppo, J. T., Malarkey, W. B., Kiecolt-Glaser, J. K., Uchino, B. N., Sgoutas-Emch, S. A., Sheridan, J. F., Berntson, G. G., & Glaser, R. (1995). Heterogeneity in neuroendocrine and immune responses to brief psychological stressors as a function of autonomic cardiac activation. *Psychosomatic Medicine, 57,* 154-164.

Cacioppo, J. T., Uchino, B. N., & Berntson, G. G. (1994). Individual differences in the autonomic origins of heart rate reactivity: The psychometrics of respiratory sinus arrhythmia and preejection period. *Psychophysiology, 31,* 412-419.

Cannon, W. B. (1928). The mechanism of emotional disturbance of bodily functions. *New England Journal of Medicine, 198,* 165-172.

Cannon, W. B. (1929). *Bodily changes in pain, hunger, fear, and rage* (2nd ed.). New York: Appleton.

Cannon, W. B. (1935). Stresses and strains of homeostasis (Mary Scott Newbold Lecture). *American Journal of Medical Sciences, 189,* 1-14.

Cannon, W. B. (1957). "Voodoo" death. *Psychosomatic Medicine, 19,* 182-190.

Carlson, N. R. (1991). *Physiology of behavior* (4th ed.). Boston: Allyn & Bacon.

Charvat, J., Dell, P., & Folkow, B. (1964). Mental factors and cardiovascular diseases. *Cardiologia, 44,* 124-141.

Churchland, P. S. (1986). *Neurophilosophy: Toward a unified science of the mind/brain.* Cambridge: MIT Press.

Cobb, S., & Rose, R. M. (1973). Hypertension, peptic ulcer, and diabetes in air traffic controllers. *Journal of the American Medical Association, 224,* 489-492.

Cohen, S. (1994). Psychosocial influences on immunity and infectious disease in humans. In R. Glaser & J. K. Kiecolt-Glaser (Eds.), *Handbook of human stress and immunity* (pp. 301-319). San Diego: Academic.

Dallman, M. F. (1993). Adaptation of the hypothalamic-pituitary-adrenal axis to chronic stress. *Trends in Endocrinology and Metabolism, 4,* 62-69.

Damasio, A. R. (1994). *Descartes' error: Emotion, reason, and the human brain.* New York: Putnam.

Descartes, R. (1956). *Discourse on method* (L. J. Lafleur, Trans.). Indianapolis, IN: Sams. (Original work published 1637)

Dodd, J., & Role, L. W. (1991). The autonomic nervous system. In E. R. Kandel, J. H. Schwartz, & T. M. Jessell (Eds.), *Principles of neural science* (3rd ed., pp. 761-775). New York: Elsevier Science.

Elstein, A. S., & Bordage, G. (1979). Psychology of clinical reasoning. In G. C. Stone, F. Cohen, & N. E. Adler (Eds.), *Health psychology—A handbook* (pp. 333-367). San Francisco: Jossey-Bass.

Engbretson, T. O., & Stoney, C. M. (1993). Cynical hostility and anger expression: Relationships to plasma lipid concentrations. *Psychosomatic Medicine, 55,* 121-122.

Engel, G. L. (1971). Sudden and rapid death during psychological stress. *Annals of Internal Medicine, 74,* 771-782.

Everson, S. A., Goldberg, D. E., Kaplan, G. A., Cohen, R. D., Pukkala, E., Tuomilehto, J., & Salonen, J. T. (1996). Hopelessness and risk of mortality and incidence of myocardial infarction and cancer. *Psychosomatic Medicine, 58,* 113-121.

Everson, S. A., Kaplan, G. A., Goldberg, D. E., & Salonen, J. T. (1996). Anticipatory blood pressure response to exercise predicts future high blood pressure in middle-aged men. *Hypertension, 27,* 1059-1064.

Everson, S. A., Kaplan, G. A., Goldberg, C. E., Salonen, R., & Salonen, J. T. (in press). Hopelessness and 4-year progression of carotid atherosclerosis: The Kuopio Ischemic Heart Disease Risk Factor Study. *Arteriosclerosis, Thrombosis, and Vascular Biology.*

Everson, S. A., Lovallo, W. R., Sausen, K. P., & Wilson, M. F. (1992). Hemodynamic characteristics of young men at risk for hypertension at rest and during laboratory stressors. *Health Psychology, 11,* 24-31.

Everson, S. A., McKey, B. S., & Lovallo, W. R. (1995). Effect of trait hostility on cardiovascular responses to harassment in young men. *International Journal of Behavioral Medicine, 2,* 172-191.

Felten, D. L., Cohen, N., Ader, R., Felten, S. Y., Carlson, S. L., & Roszman, T. L. (1991). Central-neural circuits involved in neural-immune interactions. In R. Ader, D. Felten, & N. Cohen (Eds.), *Psychoneuroimmunology* (2nd ed., pp. 3-25). San Diego: Academic.

Felten, S. Y., & Felten, D. L. (1991). Innervation of lymphoid tissue. In R. Ader, D. L. Felten, & N. Cohen (Eds.), *Psychoneuroimmunology* (2nd ed., pp. 27-69). San Diego: Academic.

FitzGerald, M. J. T. (1992). *Neuroanatomy: Basic and clinical.* London: Ballière Tindall.

Folkow, B. (1993). Physiological organization of neurohormonal responses to psychosocial stimuli: Implications for health and disease. *Annals of Behavioral Medicine, 15,* 236-244.

Foss, L., & Rothenberg, K. (1988). *The second medical revolution.* Boston: Shambhala.

Fredrikson, M., Lundberg, U., & Tuomisto, M. (1991). Serum lipid levels and cardiovascular reactivity. *Journal of Psychophysiology, 5,* 89-95.

Friedman, M., Thoresen, C. E., Gill, J. J., Ulmer, D., Powell, L. H., Price, V. A., Brown, B., Thompson, L., Rabin, D. D., Breall, W. S., Bourg, E., Levy, R., & Dixon, T. (1986). Alteration of Type A behavior and its effect on cardiac recurrences in post myocardial infarction patients: Summary results of the Recurrent Coronary Prevention Project. *American Heart Journal, 112,* 653-665.

Glaser, R., Kiecolt-Glaser, J. K., Bonneau, R., Malarkey, W., & Hughes, J. (1992). Stress-induced modulation of the immune response to recombinant Hepatitis B vaccine. *Psychosomatic Medicine, 54,* 22-29.

Glaser, R., Kiecolt-Glaser, J. K., Speicher, C. E., & Holliday, J. E. (1985). Stress, loneliness, and changes in herpesvirus latency. *Journal of Behavioral Medicine, 8,* 249-260.

Glaser, R., Rice, J., Sheridan, J., Fertel, R., Stout, J., Speicher, C., Pinsky, D., Kotur, M., Post, A., Beck, M., & Kiecolt-Glaser, J. (1987). Stress-related immune suppression: Health implications. *Brain, Behavior, and Immunity, 1,* 7-20.

Gray, J. A. (1987). *The psychology of fear and stress* (2nd ed.). Cambridge, UK: Cambridge University Press.

Gray, J. A. (1991). Neural systems, emotion and personality. In J. Madden (Ed.), *Neurobiology of learning, emotion and affect* (pp. 273-306). New York: Raven.

Guyton, A. C. (1992). *Human physiology and mechanisms of disease* (3rd ed.). Philadelphia: Saunders.

Hajjar, D. P., & Nicholson, A. C. (1995). Cellular and molecular mechanisms cause hardening of the arteries. *American Scientist, 83,* 460-467.

Hedman, A., Hjemdahl, P., Nordlander, R., & Åström, H. (1990). Effects of mental and physical stress on central haemodynamics and cardiac sympathetic nerve activity during QT interval-sensing rate-responsive and fixed rate ventricular inhibited pacing. *European Heart Journal, 11,* 903-915.

Hiley, J. D., Suomi, S. J., & Linnoila, M. (1992). A longitudinal assessment of CSF monoamine metabolites and plasma cortisol contrations in young rhesus monkeys. *Biological Psychiatry, 32,* 127-145.

Hobbs, S. (1982). Central command during exercise: Parallel activation of the cardiovascular and motor systems by descending command signals. In O. A. Smith, R. A. Galosy, & S. M. Weiss (Eds.), *Circulation, neurobiology and behavior* (pp. 217-232). New York: Elsevier.

Jansen, S. P., Nguyen, X. V., Karpitskiy, V., Mettenleiter, T. C., & Loewy, A. D. (1995). Central command neurons of the sympathetic nervous system: Basis of the fight-or-flight response. *Science, 270,* 644-646.

Jemmott, J., & Locke, S. (1984). Psychosocial factors, immunologic mediation, and human susceptibility to infectious diseases. *Psychological Bulletin, 95,* 78-108.

Jenkins, F. J., & Baum, A. (1995). Stress and reactivation of latent herpes simplex virus: A fusion of behavioral medicine and molecular biology. *Annals of Behavioral Medicine, 17,* 116-123.

Kamarck, T., & Jennings, J. R. (1991). Biobehavioral factors in sudden cardiac death. *Psychological Bulletin, 109,* 42-75.

Kaplan, J. R., Manuck, S. B., Clarkson, T. B., & Prichard, R. W. (1985). Animal models of behavioral influences on atherogenesis. In E. S. Katkin & S. B. Manuck (Eds.), *Advances in behavioral medicine*: Vol. 1 (pp. 115-164). Greenwich, CT: JAI.

Kark, J. D., Goldman, S., & Epstein, L. (1995). Iraqi missile attacks on Israel: The association of mortality with a life threatening stressor. *Journal of the American Medical Association, 273*, 1208-1210.

Kawachi, I., Colditz, G. A., Stampfer, M. J., Willett, W. C., Manson, J. E., Speizer, F. E., & Hennekens, C. H. (1995). Prospective study of shift work and risk of coronary heart disease in women. *Circulation, 92*, 3178-3182.

Keller, S. E., Shiflett, S. C., Schliefer, S. J., & Bartlett, J. A. (1994). Stress, immunity, and health. In R. Glaser & J. K. Kiecolt-Glaser (Eds.), *Handbook of human stress and immunity* (pp. 217-244). San Diego: Academic.

Kiecolt-Glaser, J. K., & Glaser, R. (1992). Psychoneuroimmunology: Can psychological interventions modulate immunity? *Journal of Consulting and Clinical Psychology, 60*, 569-575.

Kiecolt-Glaser, J. K., Malarkey, W. B., Cacioppo, J. T., & Glaser, R. (1994). Stressful personal relationships: Immune and endocrine function. In R. Glaser & J. K. Kiecolt-Glaser (Eds.), *Handbook of human stress and immunity* (pp. 321-339). San Diego: Academic.

Kiecolt-Glaser, J. K., Marucha, P. T., Malarkey, W. B., Mercado, A. M., & Glaser, R. (1995). Slowing of wound healing by psychological stress. *Lancet, 346*, 1194-1196.

Kirsch, I. (1990). *Changing expectations: A key to effective psychotherapy*. Pacific Grove, CA: Brooks/Cole.

Knardahl, S., & Hendley, E. D. (1990). Association between cardiovascular reactivity to stress and hypertension or behavior. *American Journal of Physiology, 259*, H248-H257.

Kosslyn, S. M., & Koenig, O. (1995). *Wet mind: The new cognitive neuroscience* (2nd ed.). New York: Free Press.

Kuby, J. (1994). *Immunology* (2nd ed.). New York: Freeman.

Kusnecov, A. S., & Rabin, B. S. (1994). Stressor-induced alterations of immune function: Mechanisms and issues. *International Archives of Allergy and Immunology, 105*, 107-121.

Lazarus, R. S. (1991). *Emotion and adaptation*. New York: Oxford University Press.

Lazarus, R. S., & Folkman, S. (1984). *Stress, appraisal and coping*. New York: Springer.

LeDoux, J. E. (1993). Emotional memory systems in the brain. *Behavioral Brain Research, 58*, 69-79.

Leor, J., Poole, W. K., & Kloner, R. A. (1996). Sudden cardiac death triggered by an earthquake. *New England Journal of Medicine, 334*, 413-419.

Light, K. C., Sherwood, A., & Turner, J. R. (1992). High cardiovascular reactivity to stress: A predictor of later hypertension development. In J. R. Turner, A. Sherwood, & K. C. Light (Eds.), *Individual differences in cardiovascular response to stress* (pp. 281-293). New York: Plenum.

Linden, W. (1991). What do arithmetic stress tests measure? Protocol variations and cardiovascular responses. *Psychophysiology, 28*, 91-102.

Lovallo, W. R. (1975). The cold pressor test and autonomic function: A review and integration. *Psychophysiology, 12*, 268-282.

Lovallo, W. R., Pincomb, G. A., Brackett, D. J., & Wilson, M. F. (1990). Heart rate reactivity as a predictor of neuroendocrine responses to aversive and appetitive challenges. *Psychosomatic Medicine, 52*, 17-26.

Lovallo, W. R., Pincomb, G. A., & Wilson, M. F. (1986a). Heart rate reactivity and Type A behavior as modifiers of physiological response to active and passive coping. *Psychophysiology, 23*, 105-112.

Lovallo, W. R., Pincomb, G. A., & Wilson, M. F. (1986b). Predicting response to a reaction time task: Heart rate reactivity compared with Type A behavior. *Psychophysiology, 23,* 648-656.

Lovallo, W. R., & Wilson, M. F. (1992). The role of cardiovascular reactivity in hypertension risk. In J. R. Turner, A. Sherwood, & K. C. Light (Eds.), *Individual differences in cardiovascular response to stress* (pp. 165-186). New York: Plenum.

Lovallo, W. R., Wilson, M. F., Pincomb, G. A., Edwards, G. L., Tompkins, P., & Brackett, D. (1985). Activation patterns to aversive stimulation in man: Passive exposure versus effort to control. *Psychophysiology, 22,* 283-291.

Luger, A., Deuster, P. A., Kyle, S. B., Gallucci, W. T., Montgomery, L. C., Gold, P. W., Loriaux, D. L., & Chrousos, G. P. (1987). Acute hypothalamic-pituitary-adrenal responses to the stress of treadmill exercise. *New England Journal of Medicine, 316,* 1309-1315.

Lundberg, U., & Frankenhaeuser, M. (1980). Pituitary-adrenal and sympathetic-adrenal correlates of distress and effort. *Journal of Psychosomatic Research, 24,* 125-130.

Manuck, S. B., & Garland, F. N. (1980). Stability of individual differences in cardiovascular reactivity: A thirteen month follow-up. *Physiology & Behavior, 24,* 621-624.

Manuck, S. B., Kaplan, J. R, Adams, M. R., & Clarkson, T. B. (1989). Behaviorally elicited heart rate reactivity and atherosclerosis in female cynomolgus monkeys (*Macaca fascicularis*). *Psychosomatic Medicine, 51,* 306-318.

Mason, J. W. (1968). Organization of psychoendocrine mechanisms. *Psychosomatic Medicine, 30,* 565-808.

Mason, J. W. (1975a). An historical view of the stress field: Part I. *Journal of Human Stress, 1*(1), 6-12.

Mason, J. W. (1975b). An historical view of the stress field: Part II. *Journal of Human Stress, 1*(2), 22-35.

McArdle, W. D., Foglia, G. F., & Patti, A. V. (1967). Telemetered cardiac response to selected running events. *Journal of Applied Physiology, 23,* 566-570.

McEwen, B. S., & Stellar, E. (1993). Stress and the individual: Mechanisms leading to disease. *Archives of Internal Medicine, 153,* 2093-2101.

Meaney, M. J., Bhatnagan, S., Dioria, J., Larocque, S., Francis, D., O'Donnell, D., Shanks, N., Sharma, S., Smythe, J., & Viau, V. (1993). Molecular basis for the development of individual differences in the hypothalamic-pituitary-adrenal stress response. *Cellular and Molecular Neurobiology, 13,* 321-347.

Menkes, M. S., Matthews, K. A., Krantz, D. S., Lundberg, U., Mead, L. A., Quaqish, B., Liang, K., & Thomas, C. B. (1989). Cardiovascular reactivity to the cold pressor test as a predictor of hypertension. *Hypertension, 14,* 524-530.

Miller, N. E. (1995). Clinical-experimental interactions in the development of neuroscience. *American Psychologist, 50,* 901-911.

Mittleman, M. A., Maclure, M., Sherwood, J. B., Mulry, R. P., Tofler, G. H., Jacobs, S. C., Friedman, R., Benson, H., & Muller, J. E. (1995). Triggering of acute myocardial infarction onset by episodes of anger. *Circulation, 92,* 1720-1725.

Morell, V. (1995). Zeroing in on how hormones affect the immune system. *Science, 269,* 773-775.

Munck, A., Guyre, P. M., & Holbrook, N. J. (1984). Physiological functions of glucocorticoids in stress and their relation to pharmacological actions. *Endocrine Reviews, 5,* 25-44.

Ottaway, C. A., & Husband, A. J. (1992). Central nervous system influences on lymphocyte migration. *Brain, Behavior and Immunity, 6,* 97-116.

Petrusz, P., & Merchenthaler, I. (1992). The corticotropin-releasing factor system. In C. B. Nemeroff (Ed.), *Neuroendocrinology* (pp. 129-183). Boca Raton, FL: CRC.

Plato. (1964). *The republic.* (H. D. P. Lee, Trans.) Baltimore, MD: Penguin. (Original work published ca. 380 B.C.E.)

Rushmer, R. M. (1989). Structure and function of the cardiovascular system. In N. Schneiderman, P. Kaufmann, & S. Weiss (Eds.), *Handbook of research methods in cardiovascular behavioral medicine* (pp. 5-22). New York: Plenum.

Ryle, G. (1949). *The concept of mind.* London: Hutchinson.

Saini, V., & Verrier, R. L. (1989). The experimental study of behaviorally induced arrhythmias. In N. Schneiderman, P. Kaufmann, & S. Weiss (Eds.), *Handbook of research methods in cardiovascular behavioral medicine* (pp. 51-68). New York: Plenum.

Sausen, K. P., Lovallo, W. R., Pincomb, G. A., & Wilson, M. F. (1992). Cardiovascular responses to occupational stress in medical students: A paradigm for ambulatory monitoring studies. *Health Psychology, 11,* 55-60.

Scheinman, R. I., Cogswell, P. C., Lofquist, A. K., & Baldwin, A. S. (1995). Role of transcriptional activation of IκBα in mediation of immunosuppression by glucocorticoids. *Science, 270,* 283-286.

Schulkin, J., McEwen, B. S., & Gold, P. W. (1994). Allostasis, amygdala and anticipatory angst. *Neuroscience and Biobehavioral Reviews, 18,* 385-396.

Schwartz, G. (1979). The brain as a health care system. In G. C. Stone, F. Cohen, & N. E. Adler (Eds.), *Health psychology—A handbook* (pp. 549-571). San Francisco: Jossey-Bass.

Schwartz, J. M., Stoessel, P. W., Baxter, L. R., Jr., Martin, K. M., & Phelps, M. E. (1996). Systematic changes in cerebral glucose metabolic rate after successful behavior modification treatment of obsessive-compulsive disorder. *Archives of General Psychiatry, 53,* 109-113.

Seligman, M. E. P., Maier, S., & Solomon, R. L. (1971). Unpredictable and uncontrollable aversive events. In F. R. Brush (Ed.), *Aversive conditioning and learning* (pp. 347-400). New York: Academic.

Selye, H. (1936). Thymus and adrenals in the response of the organism to injuries and intoxications. *British Journal of Experimental Pathology, 17,* 234-248.

Selye, H. (1956). *The stress of life.* New York: McGraw-Hill.

Sgoutas-Emch, S. A., Cacioppo, J. T., Uchino, B. N., Malarkey, W., Pearl, D., Kiecolt-Glaser, J. K., & Glaser, R. (1994). The effects of an acute psychological stressor on cardiovascular, endocrine, and cellular immune responses: A prospective study of individuals high and low in heart rate reactivity. *Psychophysiology, 31,* 264-271.

Sheridan, J. F., & Dobbs, C. M. (1994). Stress, viral pathogenesis, and immunity. In R. Glaser & J. Kiecolt-Glaser (Eds.), *Handbook of human stress and immunity* (pp. 101-123). San Diego: Academic.

Sherwood, A., & Turner, J. R. (1992). A conceptual and methodological overview of cardiovascular reactivity research. In J. R. Turner, A. Sherwood, & K. C. Light (Eds.), *Individual differences in cardiovascular response to stress* (pp. 3-32). New York: Plenum.

Siegman, A. W., & Smith, T. W. (Eds.). (1994). *Anger, hostility, and the heart.* Hillsdale, NJ: Lawrence Erlbaum.

Slangen, J. L., & Miller, N. E. (1969). Pharmacological tests for the function of hypothalamic norepinephrine in eating behavior. *Physiology & Behavior, 4,* 543-552.

Smith, E. E., Guyton, A. C., Manning, R. D., & White, R. J. (1976). Integrated mechanisms of cardiovascular response and control during exercise in the normal human. *Progress in Cardiovascular Diseases, 28,* 421-443.

Smith, O. A., Astley, C. A., Spelman, F. A., Golanov, E. V., Chalyan, V. G., Bowden, D. M., & Taylor, D. J. (1993). Integrating behavior and cardiovascular responses: Posture and locomotion: I. Static analysis. *American Journal of Physiology, 265,* R1458-R1468.

Smith, O. A., DeVito, J. L., & Astley, C. A. (1982). Cardiovascular control centers in the brain: One more look. In O. A. Smith, R. A. Galosy, & S. M. Weiss (Eds.), *Circulation, neurobiology and behavior* (pp. 233-246). New York: Elsevier.

Solomon, G. F., & Benton, D. (1994). Psychoneuroimmunologic aspects of aging. In R. Glaser & J. Kiecolt-Glaser (Eds.), *Handbook of human stress and immunity* (pp. 341-363). San Diego: Academic.

Spiegel, D., Bloom, J. R., Kraemer, H. C., & Gottheil, E. (1989). Effect of psychosocial treatment on survival of patients with metastatic breast cancer. *Lancet, 2,* 888-991.

Sternberg, E. M., Hill, J. M., Chrousos, G. P., Kamilaris, T., Listwak, S. J., Gold, P. W., & Wilder, R. L. (1989). Inflammatory mediator-induced hypothalamic-pituitary-adrenal axis activation is defective in streptococcal cell wall arthritis susceptible Lewis rats. *Proceedings of the National Academy of Sciences U.S.A., 86,* 2374-2378.

Sternberg, E. M., Wilder, R. L., Chrousos, G. P., & Gold, P. W. (1991). Stress responses and the pathogenesis of arthritis. In J. A. McCubbin, P. G. Kaufmann, & C. B. Nemeroff (Eds.), *Stress, neuropeptides, and systemic disease* (pp. 287-300). New York: Academic.

Stone, A. A., Neale, J. M., Cox, D. S., Napoli, A., Valdimarsdottir, H., & Kennedy-Moore, E. (1994). Daily events are associated with a secretory immune response to an oral antigen in men. *Health Psychology, 13,* 440-446.

Suarez, E. C., & Williams, R. B. (1989). Situational determinants of cardiovascular and emotional reactivity in high and low hostile men. *Psychosomatic Medicine, 51,* 404-418.

Sung, B. H., Wilson, M. F., Robinson, C., Thadani, U., & Lovallo, W. R. (1988). Mechanisms of myocardial ischemia induced by epinephrine: Comparison with exercise-induced ischemia. *Psychosomatic Medicine, 50,* 381-393.

Timio, M., Verdecchia, P., Venanzi, S., Gentili, S., Ronconi, M., Francucci, B., Montanari, M., & Bichisao, E. (1988). Age and blood pressure changes: A 20-year follow-up study in nuns in a secluded order. *Hypertension, 12,* 457-461.

Tomarken, A. J., Davidson, R. J., Wheeler, R. E., & Doss, R. C. (1992). Individual differences in anterior brain asymmetry and fundamental dimensions of emotion. *Journal of Personality and Social Psychology, 62,* 676-687.

Toulmin, S. (1967). Neuroscience and human understanding. In G. C. Quarton, T. Melnechuk, & F. O. Schmitt (Eds.), *The neurosciences: A study program* (pp. 822-832). New York: Rockefeller University Press.

Turner, J. R., & Carroll, D. (1985). Heart rate and oxygen consumption during mental arithmetic, a video game, and graded exercise: Further evidence of metabolically exaggerated cardiac adjustments? *Psychophysiology, 22,* 261-267.

Uchino, B. N., Cacioppo, R. T., Malarkey, W., & Glaser, R. (1995). Individual differences in cardiac sympathetic control predict endocrine and immune responses to acute psychological stress. *Journal of Personality and Social Psychology, 69,* 736-743.

Ungerleider, L. G. (1995). Functional brain imaging studies of cortical mechanisms for memory. *Science, 270,* 769-775.

Webster's ninth new collegiate dictionary (NeXT digital ed.). (1988). Springfield, MA: Merriam-Webster.

Weiner, H. (1991a). From simplicity to complexity (1950-1990): The case of peptic ulceration: I. Human studies. *Psychosomatic Medicine, 53,* 467-490.

Weiner, H. (1991b). From simplicity to complexity (1950-1990): The case of peptic ulceration: II. Animal studies. *Psychosomatic Medicine, 53,* 491-516.

Weiner, H. (1992). *Perturbing the organism: The biology of stressful experience.* Chicago: University of Chicago Press.

Weiss, J. M. (1970). Somatic effects of predictable and unpredictable shock. *Psychosomatic Medicine, 32,* 397-408.

Weiss, J. M. (1971a). Effects of coping behavior in different warning-signal conditions on stress pathology in rats. *Journal of Comparative and Physiological Psychology, 77,* 1-13.

Weiss, J. M. (1971b). Effects of coping behavior with and without a feedback signal on stress pathology in rats. *Journal of Comparative and Physiological Psychology, 77,* 22-30.

Weiss, J. M. (1972). Psychological factors in stress and disease. *Scientific American, 226*(6), 104-113.

Weiss, J. M. (1980). Part V: Explaining behavioral depression following uncontrollable stressful events. *Behavioral Research and Therapy, 18,* 485-504.

Weiss, J. M. (1991). Stress-induced depression: Critical neurochemical and electrophysiological changes. In J. Madden, IV (Ed.), *Neurobiology of learning, emotion and affect* (pp. 123-154). New York: Raven.

Weiss, J. M., Goodman, P. A., Losito, B. G., Corrigan, S., Charry, J. M., & Bailey, W. H. (1981). Behavioral depression produced by an uncontrollable stressor: Relationship to norepinephrine, dopamine, and serotonin levels in various regions of rat brain. *Brain Research Reviews, 3,* 167-205.

Weiss, J. M., Simson, P. G., Ambrose, M. J., Webster, A., & Hoffman, L. J. (1985). Neurochemical basis of behavioral depression. In E. S. Katkin & S. B. Manuck (Eds.), *Advances in behavioral medicine* (Vol. 1, pp. 233-276). Greenwich, CT: JAI.

Weiss, J. M., & Sundar, S. (1992). Effects of stress on cellular immune responses in animals. In A. Tasman & M. Riba (Eds.), *Review of psychiatry* (Vol. 11, pp. 145-168). Washington, DC: American Psychiatric Press.

Williams, R. B. (1994). Neurobiology, cellular and molecular biology, and psychosomatic medicine. *Psychosomatic Medicine, 56,* 308-315.

Williams, R. B., Jr., Lane, J. D., Kuhn, C. M., Melosh, W., White, A. D., & Schanberg, S. M. (1982). Type A behavior and elevated physiological and neuroendocrine responses to cognitive tasks. *Science, 218,* 483-485.

Williams, R. B. (1996, March). *Socioeconomic inequalities, health, and disease: An integrative theoretical review of potential neurobiological, psychosocial, biobehavioral, and cellular/molecular mediators.* Paper presented at the meeting of the Society of Behavioral Medicine, Washington, DC.

Wozniak, R. H. (1992). *Mind and body: René Descartes to William James.* Bethesda, MD: National Library of Medicine.

Author Index

Subject Index

About the Author

WILLIAM R. LOVALLO's research is concerned with relationships between states of stress, biological responses, and their implications for health. His current projects address cardiovascular and endocrine responses during mental stress and effects of caffeine and stress on persons at risk for hypertension. He completed his doctorate in biological psychology at the University of Oklahoma in 1978. Since that time he has served as Director of the Behavioral Sciences Laboratories at the VA Medical Center and is Professor of Psychiatry and Behavioral Sciences at the University of Oklahoma Health Sciences Center in Oklahoma City. He is also the Associate Director of the John D. and Catherine T. MacArthur Foundation's Research Network on Mind-Body Interactions. He has served on several advisory committees for the National Institutes of Health and the Veterans Administration.